"This excellent book by well-qualifie[d] [...]
very readable and understandable s[...]
tant issues in American education today."

—*Choice*

"By far and away the best and most trenchant book published on multiculturalism in years, and one of the very few that understands that language and attitudes towards language stand at the very heart of the politics of multiculturalism in the United States. Macedo and Bartolomé's book is crucial reading for anyone who cares about the current state of schools and society."

—James Paul Gee, Tashia Morgridge Professor of Reading, University of Wisconsin, Madison

"In this thought provoking text, Donaldo Macedo and Lilia Bartolomé ask us to think critically about what it means to go beyond tolerance in understanding difference. By deconstructing current debates about multicultural and bilingual education, they lay bare the ideology of exclusion that undergirds much of the discourse surrounding these topics. Writing persuasively and passionately, Macedo and Bartolomé peel away the layers that hide the raw racism in our schools and society and they demonstrate that, if we remain silent or permit the dance of bigotry to proceed, we collude in devaluating and miseducating all students."

—Sonia Nieto, University of Massachusetts, Amherst

"The ethical integrity of educators requires that they move beyond a mere discourse of culture tolerance so often embraced by mainstream teachers. The ethical integrity of educators also requires that they have the courage to recognize equality in diversity and act accordingly. In *Dancing with Bigotry*, Donaldo Macedo and Lilia I. Bartolomé demonstrate amply what it means to have courage to imagine and live in a radical cultural democracy guided by cultural respect and solidarity."

—Ramon Flecha, University of Barcelona

DANCING WITH BIGOTRY

>>> *Beyond the Politics of Tolerance*

BY DONALDO MACEDO
AND LILIA I. BARTOLOMÉ

palgrave

To our "querido hijo," Alejandro Donaldo Macedo,
who inspires us to imagine and more humane and just world.

DANCING WITH BIGOTRY
Copyright © Donald Macedo and Lilia I. Bartolomé, 1999.
All rights reserved. No part of this book may be used or reproduced in
any manner whatsoever without written permission except in the case
of brief quotations embodied in critical articles or reviews.

First published in hardcover in 1999 by St. Martin's Press
First PALGRAVE™ edition: September 2001
175 Fifth Avenue, New York, N.Y. 10010 and
Houndmills, Basingstoke, England RG21 6XS
Companies and representatives throughout the world.

PALGRAVE is the new global publishing imprint of St. Martin's Press LLC
Scholarly and Reference Division and Palgrave Publishers Ltd
(formerly Macmillan Press Ltd).

ISBN 0-312-21608-4 hardcover
ISBN 0-312-29326-7 paperback

Library of Congress Cataloging-in-Publication Data
Dancing with Bigotry : beyond the politics of tolerance /
Donaldo Macedo and Lilia Bartolomé
p. cm.
Includes bibliographical references and index.
ISBN 0-312-29326-7
1. Critical pedagogy--United States. 2. Multicultural education--
United States. I. Macedo, Donaldo P. (Donaldo Pereira), 1950-   .
II. Bartolomé, Lilia I.
LC196.5U6D26   1999
370.11'5--dc21

                                        99-27682
                                        CIP

A catalogue record for this book is available from the British Library.

Design by Adam B. Bohannon

First paperback edition: September 2001
10 9 8 7 6 5 4 3 2 1

Printed in the United States of America

CONTENTS

INTRODUCTION
Christine E. Sleeter

Multicultural education grew out of the political work of the 1960s, as African-Americans, later joined by other racial, ethnic, and cultural groups, struggled to define how and what children in the United States should be taught (Gay, 1983). In its early history, multicultural education involved: community empowerment, a challenge to low expectations for student learning, and an outrage about the absence of people of color from the curriculum. Today I find it important to situate multicultural education in this historic context, not to glorify its beginnings, but rather to direct audiences toward its embeddedness within political struggle. Although multicultural education now is known as a field within education, many people do not think of it as a site of political struggle.

In *Dancing with Bigotry: Beyond the Politics of Tolerance*, Donaldo Macedo and Lilia Bartolomé examine the connection between multicultural education and politics very closely. They challenge us to ask: How can we prepare young people, as well as teachers, to analyze events around us using a political consciousness? They ask how we can teach people to see through the ideological fog of mainstream interpretations of pluralism. Freire (1998) wrote:

[E]ven if the ideological fog has not been deliberately constructed and programmed by the dominant class, its power to obfuscate reality undeniably serves the interests of the dominant class. The dominant ideology veils reality; it makes us myopic and prevents us from seeing reality clearly. The power of the dominant ideology is always domesticating, and when we are touched and deformed by it we become ambiguous and indecisive. (6)

Events and issues are situated in particular locations and times, and acted out by particular people. Issues themselves do not come to us analyzed and interpreted, although we are constantly taught analytical perspectives. I wish to compare interpretive lenses for examining some schooling issues in Monterey County, where I live, to illustrate the power of ideological fog. The first will be a mainstream white lens, which represents the dominant viewpoint that I very often encounter when working with white educators. The second is a "human relations" multicultural lens, in which the concern is tolerance of differences. The third is a critical, political multicultural lens, which I believe is most consistent with the political struggle in which multicultural education was born, and which this book elaborates.

Who Is in the Schools?

The public schools of Monterey County, for the 1998-1999 school year, were as follows: 59 percent Latino, 28 percent white, 7 percent Asian and Pacific Islander, 4 percent African-American, and 2 percent other. About one-third of the students spoke Spanish as their first language. The teaching and administrative staff, however, was predominantly white. In 1997-1998, 73 percent of the administrators in Monterey county were white (22 percent Latino), and 78 percent of the teachers were white (15 percent Latino) (California Department of Education, October 1997). Monterey County itself is a study in contrasts. The Salinas Valley is home to the United Farm Workers founded by Cesar Chavez; field workers there are still paid very poorly and many people live in very impoverished circumstances. Pebble Beach and Carmel, on the other hand, boast some of the most expensive housing in California, and are a Mecca for tourists and well-heeled golfers. Statewide, in 1998, the median wage of Latinos was $14,560, while that of whites was $27,000.

This portrait can be read in different ways. From a mainstream white perspective, the very low wages of Latinos is due to low levels of education and high rates of immigration. The main job of schools is to improve all children's achievement levels, and as that happens, from this perspective, earnings gaps will close. The teaching and administrative staff is remarkably diverse, given that about 90 percent of the teachers in the United States are white. Also from this perspective, race and ethnicity are personal characteristics that should not matter when making professional decisions.

From a human relations multicultural perspective, these data call for a need to learn to get along. Cultural awareness celebrations are supported; ethnic holidays become the focus of multicultural curricula. Human relations advocates also see a need to learn to dialog respectfully and peacefully across differences, and invest energy in teaching peaceful conflict resolution.

From a critical multicultural perspective, however, it appears that little has changed politically for Latinos in Monterey County since the United States occupied California. California had formerly been part of Mexico, and was taken by the United States through conquest. Rodolfo Acuña (1972) wrote that "California in 1848 resembled the typical colonial situation, with the Mexicans outnumbering their new masters" (104). In 1999, Monterey County still resembles the typical colonial situation. The masters (in schools as well as other institutions) are still predominantly white, and the system works in such a way that low-wage service work is being done primarily by people of color (mostly Latino). The main beneficiaries of the system are affluent whites. The system itself, dominated by white power, is the problem. Political literacy entails learning to examine that problem and collective strategies to address it systemically. To do otherwise is to "dance with bigotry."

What Schools Teach

California, like most other states, has worked over the past decade to develop curriculum standards. In 1987, a new *History-Social Science Framework for California Public Schools* was adopted by the California State Board of Education, amid considerable controversy. Although the *Framework* claimed to be multicultural, from the perspectives of many communities of color and intellectual leaders of color, it was not (Cornbleth & Waugh, 1995; King, 1992). In 1997, the California State Board of Education readopted the *Framework*. The introduction to the

1997 edition, however, makes no mention of controversy, commenting only that "the document was received with overall enthusiasm statewide and won national recognition" (*History-Social Science Framework*, 1997, vii). Given the movement of the state toward standardizing curriculum around state frameworks, I decided to analyze this framework for myself.

First, I counted people who were named for study in the *Framework*'s course descriptions. A total of 182 individuals were named: 96 within the United States and 95 outside the United States. Of the 96 named people within the United States, 82 percent are male and 18 percent are female. They are 77 percent white, 18 percent African-American, 4 percent Native American, 1 percent Latino, and 0 percent Asian American. As the curriculum becomes more detailed and conceptually more sophisticated through the grade levels, it also becomes whiter. All of the Latino and all but one of the Native American names appear at the elementary level; at the secondary level, 79 percent of the named people are white.

Second, I examined how specific stories were told. Consider how children are to be taught how the United States acquired California. In the fourth grade curriculum, students study the history of California, as follows:

> The Mexican War for Independence should be studied and discussed. What changes did Mexico's independence from Spain bring to Alta California? By analyzing California's geography, students will see how the natural barriers and remoteness of the region influenced settlement patterns during this period . . . students will be able to put into chronological order four events that changed the course of California history: the establishment of the Bear Flag Republic, the Mexican-American War, the Gold Rush, and California's admission to statehood in 1850. These events should be studied, discussed, and analyzed. (*History-Social Science Framework*, 1997, 48)

It then goes on to suggest some analysis of Gold Rush, and to note that "the Gold Rush robbed many of California's earlier settlers of their land grants and property rights" (48). In the fifth grade curriculum,

> Maps should be used to explain how and when California, Texas, and other western lands became part of the United States. Settlement was followed by battles for independence. The war with Mexico led to cession of these territories, which then became states. These events provide important opportunities to focus on Hispanic people of California and the Southwest, on the effects of these events on their lives, and on their distinctive contributions to American culture. (55)

The eighth grade curriculum again takes up the question of how the Southwest became a part of the United States:

> Students should study the northward movement of settlers from Mexico into the great Southwest, with emphasis on the locations of Mexican settlements, their cultural traditions, their attitudes toward slavery, their land-grant system, and the economy they established in these regions. Students need this background before they can analyze the events that followed the arrival of westward-moving settlers from the East into these Mexican territories. Special attention should be given to the Mexican-American War, its territorial settlements, and its aftermath in the lives of the Mexican families who first lived in the region. (71)

From a mainstream white perspective, this curriculum reflects a reasonable historical analysis that teaches children to use tools of geography to understand historical events. The curriculum is dominated by whites because U.S. history has been made largely by people of European descent, but there is room in this curriculum to acknowledge Mexican cultural contributions to the United States. After students have learned U.S. history as a whole, they can study Mexican American history if they wish.

From a human relations multicultural perspective, this curriculum provides spaces for cultural celebration. Although children should know about past wars, curricula should emphasize the "positive" dimensions of cultural diversity more than the "negative" dimensions. So, past wars and conflicts might be down played, but attention devoted to Mexican cultural traditions when these historic events are studied.

From a political multicultural perspective, this rendering of history teaches "ideological fog" (Freire, 1998). In this telling of how the northern half of Mexico became part of the United States, conquest is not mentioned, nor is how students might "analyze the events that followed the arrival of Westward moving settlers from the East." The great Southwest is not explicitly stated as being part of Mexico, but rather as receiving settlers from Mexico, wording that suggests an immigration paradigm for Mexicans, rather than a colonial paradigm. Mexican dispossession in the process of colonization is attributed to abstractions like "the Gold Rush" rather than to the specific actions of people; cession from Mexico is attributed to the abstraction of war rather than the actions of Anglos. One can consider the teaching of this history to students, the majority of whom in Monterey County are Latino, as propaganda designed to subvert any community-based historical memories that question the legitimacy of white dominance in California.

Assessing Student Achievement

In April 1999, I visited an elementary classroom while a state-mandated writing test was being given. In this classroom, the great majority of the students were of Mexican descent, most of them speaking Spanish as their first language. There were also several African-American students and one Anglo student. The class was being taught in English; the teacher was Anglo and did not speak Spanish. For this test, students were to write a letter in English to an imaginary friend. The teacher was to lead them through a preliminary brainstorming, then they had almost an hour to write. In this particular class, most of the students finished within a few minutes. Many had written little more than a sentence, or a few phrases. As I looked at their papers, it was clear that most would fail the test. Both the teacher and I found it very painful to have to watch these children being put through a high-stakes exercise in which they were demonstrating failure. In Monterey County, many public schools scored below the national mean, and educators are scrambling for plans to reform the schools in order to raise student achievement.

The reform discussions at the administrative level are taking place largely within a "back to basics" discourse. Bilingual education has been significantly weakened following passage of Proposition 227, and since the tests are in English, most reform discussions assume rapid transition into English as a desirable goal. From a mainstream white perspective, multicultural education is simply irrelevant to the problem of how to raise achievement scores.

From a human relations multicultural perspective, the emphasis on testing diverts us from teaching and from appreciating differences. Many teachers I have talked with are angry at having to administer tests they know their students will perform poorly on, and regard this as taking away valuable teaching time. Further, the emphasis on testing is reducing support for spending time developing social skills and self-esteem. In a climate of increased testing, the "whole child" gets ignored.

From a political multicultural perspective, high stakes testing, using standardized tests given in English over the standardized curriculum ends up framing children of color and poor white children as deficient. High stakes testing in English has framed Spanish as a problem to overcome rather than a language resource on which to build. The tests solidify the institutionalization of an ideologically conservative, white dominant curriculum. Relatively affluent white communities tend to see relatively poor communities of color as lacking in knowledge and as sources of problems (such as gangs and poverty), in any case. High-stakes testing, with results published in the newspaper, confirms that perspective. Although the testing may result in more attention being given to low-achieving students, it doesn't change the relative position of groups of students. In other words, standardized curricula with standardized testing has not led to parity of achievement and power among groups. Nor is it designed to do that.

Beyond the Politics of Tolerance

These examples have tried to illustrate ways in which mainstream white interpretations of current issues have the effect of continuing a history of oppressive relations. An alternative perspective—multicultural education as human relations—sidesteps the history of colonialism and today's power struggles, by attempting to put a happy face on "diversity." These two perspectives, which are not mutually exclusive, are the ones I most frequently encounter when working with educators. They lead to, as Macedo and Bartolomé point out in Chapter Five, making a fetish of teaching methods, and resist attempts to see connections between teaching methods and politics.

But while I am very critical of mainstream and human relations perspectives, I share with Macedo and Bartolomé a hope for change. I have worked with many students and teachers over the years who have learned to see events with political clarity, to question relations of domination as they are played out locally, and to recognize and support community-based struggles for liberation. In my experience there is no formula for transforming a person's perspective, but encountering political analyses such as those presented in this book greatly helps. *Dancing with Bigotry* presents excellent analyses of issues, always drawing the reader back to the question of political ideology embedded in education, and vision for the future.

Williams (1991) wrote of the United States: "From the beginning, our imperial way of life seduced us into assuming that we could go on forever projecting the present into the future: that we could start over and over again. . . . Our intellectual, political, and psychological confusion is the result of our ahistorical faith that we are now and never have been an empire" (71). He incisively analyzes U.S. history to build a case that for Americans, empire has become "a way of life." But he concludes: "Do you want to imagine a new America or do you want to preserve the empire? Now, as surely we all know, preserving the empire is an exercise in futility. We will sizzle or suffocate. So let us get on with imagining a new America. Once we imagine it, break out of the imperial idiom, we just might be able to create a nonimperial America" (102).

Let us join Donaldo Macedo and Lilia Bartolomé in imagining a new, nonimperial America. Let us stop dancing with bigotry.

REFERENCES

Acuña, R. 1972. *Occupied America: The Chicano's Struggle toward Liberation*. San Francisco: Canfield Press.

Cornbleth, C. & Waugh, D. 1995. *The Great Speckled Bird: Multicultural Politics and Education Decision-making*. New York: St. Martins Press.

Freire, P. 1998. *Teachers as Cultural Workers*. Boulder, CO: Westview Press.

Gay, G. 1983. "Multiethnic Education: Historical Developments and Future Prospects." *Phi Delta Kappan* 64, pp. 560-563.

History-Social Science Framework for California Public Schools. 1997. Sacramento, CA: California Department of Education.

King, J. E. 1992. "Diaspora Literacy and Consciousness in the Struggle against Miseducation in the Black Community." *Journal of Negro Education* 61 (3): 317-340.

Williams, W. A. 1991. "Empire as a Way of Life." *Radical History* 50, 71-102.

CHAPTER 1

DANCING WITH BIGOTRY
The Poisoning of Racial and Ethnic Identities

*I concluded long ago that they found the color of my skin
inhibitory. This color seems to operate as a most disagreeable
mirror, and a great deal of one's energy is expended in reassuring
white Americans that they do not see what they see.*

*This is utterly futile, of course, since they do see what they see.
And what they see is an appallingly oppressive and bloody history
known all over the world. What they see is a disastrous, continuing, present condition which menaces them, and for which they
bear an inescapable responsibility. But since in the main they
seem to lack the energy to change this condition they would not
be reminding of it.*

—*James Baldwin*[1]

As James Baldwin so succinctly points out, many white Americans
prefer not to be reminded of the "appallingly oppressive and bloody
history" of racism that has characterized the very fabric of U. S. society. In fact many, if not most, white Americans from various ethnic
backgrounds would feel extremely uncomfortable if the curriculum in
schools incorporated an antiracist pedagogy that asked, "Mirror, mirror on the wall, is everyone welcome in the hall?"

Sadly, in a good number of halls not everyone is welcome. A report
published by the National Association of Black Journalists revealed
that 32 percent of African-American journalists fear that bringing up
issues of race in their articles damages their chances for advancement.[2] This statistic reveals a condition of fear that most likely exists
in many forms and many occupations, including teaching. We believe

this condition of fear gives rise to a form of censorship that views the aggressive denouncement of racism as worse than the racist act itself.

In this chapter, we argue that, as the end of the century draws closer, one of the most pressing challenges facing educators in the United States is the specter of an "ethnic and cultural war," which constitutes, in our view, a code phrase that engenders our society's licentiousness toward racism. We use the examples from the mass media, popular culture, and politics to illustrate the larger situations facing educators, how this type of argument is both ignored in much of the academic research and rhetoric, and why taking on the sources of "mass public education" is essential. Academia needs to understand that the popular press and the mass media educate more people about issues regarding ethnicity and race than all other sources of education available to U.S. citizens. By shunning the mass media, educators are missing the obvious: that is, that more public education is done by the media than by teachers, professors, and anyone else. This would serve to further develop the links between the issues discussed so far and education.

Although our chapter sheds light on the ideological mechanisms that shape and maintain our racist social order, we move our discussion beyond the reductionistic binarism of white versus black racism. Thus we not only avoid falling prey to a binaristic approach to race analysis, but also differentiate ethnic from racial groups in order to avoid the facile interpretation of these ideological constructs. What is important, we believe, is the development of a critical comprehension of the relationship between the ideological constructs that determine and shape racial and ethnic realities. However, the fragmentation of ethnic and racial realities is part of the social organization of knowledge defined rigidly along disciplinary boundaries, which often results in the study of a single group under the rubric "ethnicity." This fragmentation represents a rupture of ethnic and racial relations, and propagates an ideology that creates and sustains false dichotomies delineated by ethnic or racial disciplinary boundaries. We believe that racism is an ideological construct that interpenetrates both ethnic and racial realities. An analysis of racism isolated from other ideological categories along the lines of ethnicity, class, gender, and culture does little good. Only by a process through which the dominant white ideology is deconstructed can we begin to understand the intimate relationships among the asymmetrical distributions of power and privilege among different ethnic and racial groups, including lower-class ethnic whites. In other words, we need to avoid the lumping of multiple identities into a monolithic entity such as race or ethnicity.

It is important to point out that the analysis of race, ethnicity, and gender as if they were monolithic entities prevents us from understanding that these categories represent interpenetrating realms of a shared dominant ideological foundation. In the case of gender, for example, bell hooks argues that "sexism, racism, and class exploitation constitute interlocking systems of domination . . . sex, race, and class, and not sex alone, determine the nature of any female's identity status, and circumstance, the degree to which she will or will not be dominated, the extent to which she will have the power to dominate."[3]

The same can be argued for race and ethnicity. As part of a broader struggle to fight oppression of all forms, race and ethnicity need to be understood as ideological constructs that historically have served the purpose of perpetuating racism and as political categories that can function to mobilize resistance against white domination. In the latter case, both racial and ethnic identities take on positive values as they contribute to the struggle for social justice and the eradication of oppression. As ideological constructs, both race and ethnicity are separated from class and gender issues so as to prevent the understanding of the interconnecting relationship hidden in the dominant white ideology.

Part of the deconstruction of dominant white ideology involves understanding how ethnicity and race interpenetrate each other, in what Pepi Leistyna refers to as "racenicity, a process through which the ideological construction of race has a significant impact on ethnicity."[4] We need to move beyond a discourse that views difference as simply aesthetic or as separate categories of analysis. We must link difference to questions of power, where racial categories, among other characteristics, are treated as political categories that do not exist in a power vacuum. These categories exist in relation to one another, mediated always by asymmetrical power relationships. According to Stanley Aronowitz:

> The concept of ethnicity with respect to education expresses two somewhat different characteristics of how issues of inequality are conventionally addressed in the literature. Recently, descriptively, the term has been employed to discuss issues of access and since we have no social scientifically acceptable discourse of class, ethnicity has become the displacement of this largely unacknowledged aspect of educational access and performance.[5]

The challenge for educators is to interrogate the descriptive nature of the discourse on race and ethnicity in order to unveil how the description hides the fact that "ethnicity has become the displacement" of class. Educators need to understand how "cultural differences are purged and social practices are reshaped around a racial identity, [giving rise to] a hierarchy that subcategorizes while devaluing groups of people that are designated 'racial others,' 'ethnics,' 'outsiders.'"[6]

Central to the idea of an ethnic and cultural war is the creation of an ideologically coded language that serves at least two fundamental functions: on the one hand, this language veils the racism that characterizes U.S. society, and on the other hand, it insidiously perpetuates both ethnic and racial stereotypes that devalue identities of resistance and struggle. Although the present assault on Latinos is mostly characterized by a form of racism at the level of language, it is important to differentiate between language as racism and the experience of racism. For example, former presidential candidate Patrick Buchanan's call for the end of illegal immigration "even if it means putting the National Guard all along the Southern frontier" constitutes a form of racism at the level of language.[7] This language-based racism has had the effect of licensing institutional discrimination, whereby both documented and undocumented immigrants materially experience the loss of their dignity, the denial of their humanity, and, in many cases, outright violence, as witnessed by the recent cruel beatings of a Mexican man and woman by the border patrol. This incident was captured on videotape, and outraged the Latino/Mexicano communities in the United States, as well as in Mexico, leading to a number of demonstrations in Los Angeles. Terms like "border rats," "wetbacks," "aliens" "illegals," "welfare queens," and "nonwhite hordes" used by the popular press not only dehumanize other cultural beings but also serve to justify the violence perpetuated against subordinate groups.

Racist language is one example of what Pierre Bourdieu refers to as "the hegemony of symbolic violence."[8] As educators, we need to understand fully the interrelationship between symbolic violence produced through language and the essence of the experience of racism. While the two are not mutually exclusive, "language also constitutes and mediates the multiple experiences of identity by both historicizing it and revealing its partiality and incompleteness, its limits are realized in the material nature of experience as it names the body through the specificity of place, space, and history."[9] This is very much in line with John Fiske's notion that "there is a material experience of homelessness ... but the boundary between the two cannot be drawn sharply. Material conditions are inescapably saturated with culture and, equally, cultural conditions are inescapably experienced as material."[10]

By deconstructing the cultural conditions that give rise to the present violent assault on undocumented immigrants, affirmative action, African-Americans, and other racial and ethnic groups, we can single out those ideological factors that enable even highly educated individuals to embrace blindly, for example, conservative radio talk-show host Rush Limbaugh's racist tirades designed to demonize and dehumanize ethnic and cultural identities other than his own. Here are some examples:

- Now I got something for you that's true—1992, Tufts University, Boston. This is 24 years ago or 22 years ago. Three-year study of 5,000 coeds, and they used a benchmark of a bra size of 34C. They forward that—now wait! It's true. The larger the bra size, the smaller the IQ.

- Feminism was established so that unattractive women could have easier access to mainstream society.
- There are more American Indians alive today than there were when Columbus arrived or at any other time in history. Does that sound like a record of genocide?
- Taxpaying citizens are not being given access to these welfare and health services that they deserve and desire. But if you're an illegal immigrant and cross the border, you get everything you want.[11]

The racism and high level of xenophobia we are witnessing in our society today are not caused by isolated acts by individuals such as Limbaugh or onetime Louisiana gubernatorial candidate David Duke. Rather, these individuals are representatives of an orchestrated effort by segments of the dominant society to wage a war on the poor and on people who, by virtue of their race, ethnicity, language, and class, are reduced at best to half-citizens, and at worst to a national enemy responsible for all the ills afflicting our society. We need to understand the cultural and historical context that gives rise to over 20 million Limbaugh "ditto heads" who tune in to his weekly radio and television programs.

We need also to understand those ideological elements that inform our policymakers and those individuals who shape public opinion by supporting and rewarding Limbaugh's unapologetic demonizing of other cultural subjects. For example, television commentator Ted Koppel considers him "very smart. He does his homework. He is well informed." Syndicated columnist George Will considers him the "fourth branch of government," and former Secretary of Education William Bennett—the virtue man—describes Limbaugh as "possibly our greatest living American."[12] What remains incomprehensible is why highly educated individuals like Koppel, Will, and Bennett cannot see through Limbaugh's obvious distortions of history and falsification of reality. We posit that the inability to perceive distinctions and falsifications of reality is partly due to the hegemonic forces that promote an acritical education via the fragmentation of bodies of knowledge. Such a process makes it very difficult for students (and the general population) to make connections among historical events so as to gain a more critical understanding of reality. The promotion of an acritical education was evident when David Spritzler, a twelve-year-old student at Boston Latin School, faced disciplinary action for his refusal to recite the Pledge of Allegiance, which he considered "a hypocritical exhortation to patriotism" in that there is not "liberty and justice for all." According to Spritzler, the pledge is an attempt to unite:

> [the] oppressed and oppressors. You have people who drive nice cars, live in nice houses, and don't have to worry about money. Then you have the poor people, living in bad neighborhoods and going to bad schools. Somehow the Pledge makes it seem that everybody's equal when that's not happening. There is no justice for everybody.[13]

Spritzler's teachers' and administrators' inability to see the obvious hypocrisy contained in the Pledge of Allegiance represents what Noam Chomsky calls "a real sign of deep indoctrination [in] that you can't understand elementary thoughts that any ten-year-old can understand. That's real indoctrination. So for him [the indoctrinated individual], it's kind of like a theological truth, a truth of received religion."[14]

Against these cruel and racist cultural conditions, we can begin to understand that it is not a coincidence that Patrick Buchanan reiterated in his first presidential campaign platform that his fellow Americans should "wage a cultural revolution in the nineties as sweeping as the political revolution of the eighties."[15] In fact, this cultural revolution is indeed moving forward with rapid speed, from the onslaught on cultural diversity and multicultural education to Patrick Buchanan's call to U.S. national and patriotic sense to build a large wall to keep the "illegals" in Mexico. Some might claim that Patrick Buchanan's vicious attack on immigrants could be interpreted in ways other than as racism. If that were the case, how could we explain his unfortunate testament: "I think God made all people good, but if we had to take a million immigrants—in say Zulus next year or Englishmen—and put them in Virginia, what group would be easier to assimilate and would cause less problems for the people of Virginia?"[16]

It is the same U.S. national and patriotic sense that allowed President Clinton not to be outdone by the extreme right's forcing him to announce in his 1995 State of the Union address that:

All Americans, not only in the states most heavily affected, but in every place in this country, are rightly disturbed by the large numbers of illegal aliens entering our country. The jobs they hold might otherwise be held by citizens or legal immigrants. The public services they use impose burdens on our taxpayers. That's why our administration has moved aggressively to secure our borders more by hiring a record number of new border guards, by deporting twice as many criminal aliens as ever before, by cracking down on illegal hiring, by barring welfare benefits to illegal aliens.

In the budget I will present to you, we will try to do more to speed the deportation of illegal aliens who are arrested for crimes, to better identify illegal aliens in the workplace as recommended by the commission headed by former Congresswoman Barbara Jordan."[17]

A close analysis of the Republican attack on immigrants and cultural groups and our liberal Democratic president's remarks during his State of the Union Address confirm what has been for decades the United States's best-kept secret: there is no critical ideological difference between the Republican and Democratic parties. Ideologically speaking, in the United States we have a one-party system of government represented by two branches with only cosmetic differences, cloaked in the guise of Republicans and Democrats.

We believe that the same racist sentiment enabled President Clinton to abandon the nomination of Lani Guinier to head the Justice Department's Civil Rights Division because she demonstrated in her writings that the working-class poor, African-Americans, and members of other minority cultural groups do not have representation in the white-male-dominated two-party system and that the system in fact, fueled by a capitalist ideology, works aggressively against the interests of these groups. It is again the same racist ideology that is pushing President Clinton to join the chorus calling for an end to affirmative action policies, even though the benefactors of de facto affirmative action through the good-old-boy networks since the birth of this country have been white males, who continue to dominate all sectors of institutional and economic life in this society. For example, according to employment data on Boston banks from the Equal Employment Opportunity Commission:

From 1990-1993, the industry added 4,116 jobs. While the percentage of white male officers and managers rose by 10 percent, the percentage of African-American officers and managers dropped by 25 percent. While the percentage of white female clerical workers went up 10 percent, the percentage of African-American clerical workers dropped 15 percent.[18]

"Affirmative action" and "welfare" are also code words that license a form of racism via language that assuages the fear of the White working and middle class as they steadily lose ground to the real "affirmative action and welfare" programs designed to further enrich the upper class and big business:

When the Fed raises the interest rates, it helps big business at the expense of individual home owners. When politicians resist raising the minimum wage, it helps big business send off the working poor. When politicians want liability caps, they defend Big Oil, Ma Bell and her offspring and Detroit gas guzzlers over potential victims of defective products and pollution. As the Gingrich revolution slashes school lunches for the poor, corporations get $1.11 billion in tax breaks, according to Labor secretary Robert Reich.[19]

We also know that even within the context of the present affirmative action policy, the genuine beneficiaries have been white women. Their convenient silence on the present assault on affirmative action makes them complicit in perpetuating the racist myth that

black people take jobs from white people . . . [which leads] one
to conclude that African-Americans are not considered Americans. White men lose jobs to other white men who do not say,
they gave my job to an inferior white man! White male competency is assumed. African-Americans, regardless of achievement, are forever on trial[20]

In other words, Henry Louis Gates Jr.'s prominence as a scholar
did not lessen the racism he had to face at Duke University when he
taught there. Cornel West's status as a renowned public intellectual
did little for him as he watched nine taxis go by and refuse to pick him
up in the streets of New York. bell hooks's eminence as a major feminist scholar does not lessen the pain of racism and sexism she
endures; her status as an author of many highly acclaimed feminist
books still does not provide her with the access to media and maga-
zines enjoyed by many white feminists. As hooks recently pointed out
to Naomi Wolf:

> I have written eight feminist books. None of the magazines that
> have talked about your book, Naomi, have ever talked about my
> books at all. Now, that's not because there aren't ideas in my
> books that have universal appeal. It's because the issue that you
> raised in *The Beauty Myth* is still about beauty. We have to
> acknowledge that all of us do not have equal acces.[21]

hooks's comment denudes the myth created by the anti-affirmative
action discourse that "pretends that we live in a colorblind society
where individuals are treated according to the American ethic [that]
has always held that individual effort and achievement are valued and
rewarded."[22]

The separation of the individual from the collective consciousness
is part of the dominant white ideology's mechanism to fragment reality, which makes it easier for individuals to accept living within the lie
that we exist in a raceless and color-blind society. The real issue
behind the present assault on multiculturalism and affirmative action
is that we must never fall prey to a pedagogy of big lies.[23] The funda-

mental challenge for Americans in general, and educators in particular, is to accept Derrick Bell's call for a "continuing quest for new directions in our struggle for racial justice, a struggle we must continue even if . . . racism is an integral, permanent and indestructible component of this society."[24]

Poisoning Racial and Ethnic Identities

Accepting bell's challenge, we point out that the real issue is not Western civilization versus multiculturalism or affirmative action versus individual effort and merit. Cultural dominance and racism are the hidden issues that inform the pernicious debate on cultural diversity and its ramifications, such as affirmative action. We cannot speak of our American "common culture" and democracy in view of the quasi-apartheid conditions that have relegated American Indians to reservations, created ghettos, and supported the affirmative action of redlining and Robin Hood policies in reverse. How can we honestly accept the mythical reality of our common culture when its major proponents are simultaneously engaged in a permanent process of putting other cultural identities on trial? A willingness to negate the contributions of subordinated groups can be easily detected in the comments of John Silber, former Boston University president and present chairman of the Massachusetts State Board of Education, who, during his campaign for governor of Massachusetts in 1990 asked: "Why has Massachusetts suddenly become so popular for people who are accustomed to living in a tropical climate? Amazing. There has got to be a welfare magnet going on here, and right now I am making a study to find out what that magnet is. Why should Lowell be the Cambodian capital of America?"[25]

If John Silber had conducted his study as promised, he would soon realize how he dances with bigotry, since the majority of welfare recipients in Lowell, Massachusetts, are not Cambodians, but white Americans. He would also learn that the Asian community in Lowell represents a real economic force, filling the gaps made by the flight of jobs and capital that have left Lowell struggling with an urban decay like that of other old industrial cities. It is the same dance with bigotry that now informs our politicians in their quest for higher offices, including the presidency.

David Duke, a Republican candidate in the 1990 presidential primaries, minced no words when he stated: "America is being invaded by hordes of dusty third world peoples, and with each passing hour our economic well-being, cultural heritage, freedom, and racial roots are being battered into oblivion."[26]

He continues his demonization of the "other" cultural and ethnic subjects, stating: "It's them! They're what's wrong with America! They're taking your job, soaking up your tax dollars, living off food stamps, drinking cheap wine and making babies at our expense."[27]

These racist sentiments are not lost in the proliferation of conservative radio talk shows, like Rush Limbaugh's, whose major purpose is to exacerbate the racist fabric of our society. The agenda of such shows is apparent in a local talk show broadcast in Brockton, Massachusetts, in which a caller remarked: "Why should we be supporting these bilinguals? We should take care of our own first. The problem with Brockton is the Haitians, the Hispanics, the Cape Verdeans that are ruining our neighborhood."[28]

Although these examples point to racism at the level of language, the relationship between racist statements and the effects on people's lives is direct. For example, while California governor Pete Wilson and other politicians made speeches using a kind of language that demonized so-called illegal immigrants, the actual experience of racism became immeasurably worse with the passage of Proposition 187 in California. In fact, Proposition 187 can be viewed as a precursor in a pattern of assault on subordinated groups that culminated with the passage in November 1996 of Proposition 209, which proposed to end affirmative action in California. The cultural condition that led to the passage of these laws, which were designed to control the flow of illegal immigrants and to end affirmative action in California, has had the effect of licensing institutional discrimination whereby both legal and illegal immigrants materially experience the loss of their dignity, the denial of human citizenship, and, in many cases, outright violent and criminal acts committed by those institutions responsible for implementing the law. According to Human Rights Watch/Americas: "The politically charged drive to curb illegal immigration may be coming at a serious price: beatings, shootings, rapes and death of aliens at the hand of the US Border Patrol."[29]

As anti-immigrant sentiment grows stronger, the Immigration and Naturalization Service (INS) plans to increase its force from 4,200 to 7,000 by 1998, with few safeguards in place to ensure that the new hires will not continue to increase the human rights abuses perpetrated along the U.S. Mexican border. As Allyson Collins of Human Rights Watch/Americas notes, the "anti-immigrant sentiment dims the hope of safeguarding aliens as the United States fortifies its border. These are very unpopular victims."[30] Not only is there no guarantee that the INS will protect the rights of human beings who have already been dehumanized as "aliens" or "illegals," but this dehumanizing process has also been met by an unsettling silence, even among liberals. This is not entirely surprising, given the liberals' paradoxical posture with respect to race issues. On the one hand, liberals progressively idealize "principles of liberty, equality, and fraternity [while insisting] upon the moral irrelevance of race. Race is irrelevant, but all is race."[31] On the other hand, some liberals accept the notion of difference and call for ways in which difference is tolerated. For example, there is a rapid growth of textbooks ostensibly designed to teach racial and multicultural tolerance. But what these texts in fact do is hide the asymmetrical distribution of power and cultural capital through a form of paternalism that promises to the "other" a dose of tolerance. In other words, since we coexist and must find ways to get along, I will tolerate you. Missing from this posture is the ethical position that calls for mutual respect and even racial and cultural solidarity. As David Goldberg argues, tolerance "presupposes that its object is morally repugnant, that it really needs to be reformed, that is, altered."[32] Accordingly, racial and cultural tolerance practiced by the dominant sectors within U.S. society may view this form of tolerance as a process through which the different "other" is permitted to think, or at least hope, that through this so-called tolerance, the intolerable features that characterize the different "other" will be eliminated or repressed. Thus, Goldberg is correct in pointing out that

> liberals are moved to overcome the racial differences they toler-
> ate and have been so instrumental in fabricating by diluting
> them, by bleaching them out through assimilation or integra-
> tion. The liberal would assume away the difference in other-
> ness, maintaining thereby the dominance of a presumed
> sameness, the universally imposed similarity in identity. The
> paradox is perpetrated: the commitment to tolerance turns only
> on modernity's natural inclination to intolerance; acceptance of
> otherness presupposes as it at once necessitates delegitimiza-
> tion of the other.[33]

Tolerance for different racial and ethnic groups as proposed by some white liberals not only constitutes a veil behind which they hide their racism, it also puts them in a compromising racial position. While calling for racial tolerance, a paternalistic term, they often maintain the privilege that is complicit with the dominant ideology. In other words, the call for tolerance never questions the asymmetrical power relations that give them their privilege. Thus, many white liber-als willingly call and work for cultural tolerance but are reluctant to confront issues of inequality, power, ethics, race, and ethnicity in a way that could actually lead to social transformation that would make society more democratic and humane and less racist and discrimina-tory. This form of racism is readily understood by its victims, as observed by Carol Swain, an African-American professor at Princeton University: "White liberals are among the most racist people I know; they're so patronizing towards blacks."[34]

Against this landscape of racism, it becomes difficult to argue that these positions are taken only by fringe individuals such as David Duke. As hard as we may want to stretch the truth, we cannot forget that he has been elected to public office in Louisiana. Nor can we argue that John Silber is on the fringe. He is as mainstream as those Republicans who signed on with the Contract with America, propos-ing to cut lunch programs for poor children, take away cash assistance to unwed mothers with dependent children, tighten fuel assistance to the elderly, abolish the food stamp program, and crack down on illegal immigrants while denying social benefits to legal immigrants. In short, the racism and xenophobia we are witnessing in our society today are not isolated acts of individuals on the fringe.

It is against this mean-spirited and racist backdrop that we analyze the controversy over multiculturalism and the role that language plays in the process. In our analysis we do not discuss the way Puerto Ricans dance salsa, how Chicanos celebrate Cinco de Mayo, or how Haitians believe in voodoo. Although the knowledge of such cultural traits is useful, we do not think it prepares us to deal with the tensions and contradictions generated by the coexistence of multicultural groups in a racist society. Instead, we argue that multicultural analyses should not be limited to the study of the "other" in a way that makes the white cultural group invisible and beyond study. White invisibility is achieved partly through the very language we use to structure our discourse on race and ethnicity. For example, both whites and nonwhite racial and ethnic groups use the linguistic construction "people of color" to designate non white individuals. The hidden assumption is that white is colorless, a proposition that is semantically impossible. By pointing out that white is also a color, we can begin to interrogate the false assumptions that strip white people of their ethnicity. In fact, a thorough understanding of racial and ethnic realities must begin by reinserting both color and ethnicity into the false discourse of colorless whites that contributes to making ethnicity invisible within this concept of whiteness. In addition, it is not necessarily important for us to understand how cultural differences are structured along specific behavior patterns, but it is important to understand instead the antagonism and tensions engendered by cultural differences that coexist asymmetrically in terms of power relations.

Culture is intertwined with language and represents a sizable dimension of its reality, but language is rarely studied as part of our multicultural understanding. In this country we often take for granted that the study of multiculturalism should be done in English only; in addition, we also rarely question the role of the dominant language in the devaluation of the cultural and ethnic groups under study. Put simply, we understand little how the English language can subordinate and alienate members of the cultures we study through English. We need to understand how English masks the web of ideological manipulation that makes white cultural and ethnic groups invisible and outside the realm of study. Hence, language not only produces cultural and social inequalities but is also used by the dominant white ideology to distort and falsify realities. Take the proposition "school choice," which creates the illusion that all parents can equally exercise their democratic right to choose the best schools for their children.

The illusion of choice also reinforces the myth that every American can choose where to live and work. However, for a group of African-Americans who attempted to implement the court-ordered integration of a public housing complex in Vidor, Texas, the myth soon became a nightmare. Despite their efforts to assimilate quietly, they were subjected for months to Ku Klux Klan threats and racial epithets shouted from passing cars. Unable to endure the unremittingly hostile atmosphere, they decided to leave.

The illusion of choice also creates a pedagogy of entrapment that makes it undemocratic to argue against school choice. Thus school choice becomes part of a discourse that brooks no dissension or argument, for to argue against it is to deny democracy. The hidden curriculum of school choice consists of taking precious resources from poor schools that are on the verge of bankruptcy to support private or well-to-do public schools. For example, at the same time that the Brockton, Massachusetts public schools terminated the contract of 120 teachers due to a draconian budget cut, the system shifted approximately $1 million to support middle-class Brockton students who chose to enroll in the more affluent Avon public schools nearby. Although the Avon schools benefited greatly from the school choice windfall, they did not welcome equally all students from Brockton. When a Brockton special education student decided to defy his rejection by the Avon schools, the principal stood by the door on the first day of class to prevent this student, accompanied by his parents, from entering the school building. This episode provides a glimpse of possible future behavior by the Avon schools if a large number of Brockton's subordinated students pick an Avon school as their school of choice. The school choice discourse also eclipses the more fundamental issue of educational funding inequity.

Using language as a mirror, we can begin to understand U.S. society's pathological need to demonize the "other" so as to have an enemy to blame for all its ills. During the 1950s, 1960s, and 1970s, we used communism to represent all the evils that needed to be confronted. This gave rise to a dark chapter in our history that not only threatened the civil liberties guaranteed by our Constitution but also flirted with the totalitarian impulses of McCarthyism, which differed little from the police states we were denouncing. With the fall of the Berlin Wall, President Bush replaced the communist threat with the War on Drugs, a war that is associated mostly with subordinated groups to the extent that they have been framed as a point of reference for the drug problem. This is evident in the disproportionate number of African-Americans and Latinos who have been sentenced to jail on drug charges. In fact, the laws that regulate penalties for drug offenses clearly reflect biases against subordinated groups. For example, penalties for possession of cocaine, which is often referred to as a "white drug," are less strict than the penalties given for the possession of the much less expensive cocaine by-product crack, which is more readily found in poor inner-city neighborhoods. The drug war has been used to rationalize the presence of U.S. troops in many Latin American countries, including Colombia, Peru, Bolivia, and Guatemala, to fight and destroy coca fields and drug laboratories. The U.S. government has refused to realize that the only effective way to fight the war on drugs is to decrease demand. In order to decrease demand, we would need a profound social transformation that goes far beyond Nancy Reagan's empty slogan of "Just Say No." Even law enforcement officials and officials of these Latin American countries have admitted that they are losing the drug war. In fact, by focusing only on the elimination of drug production, we ignore the social causes that breed a high demand for drugs. In addition, by focusing on drug production, the government can distract the public from the allegation in the media that the CIA played an important role in introducing drugs in South Los Angeles in order to help finance the Contra War in Nicaragua, while keeping the African American and Latino communities sedated. According to Mary Kimbrough, the owner of an African arts and books store, the CIA drug link in Los Angeles "fits a historical pattern of racism by the American government designed to keep us in a permanent underclass."[35] In fact, if we look back in history, we soon realize that Kimbrough's statement is not merely part of a conspiracy theory. For instance, Benjamin Franklin, in his autobiography, had no shame when he stated that "indeed if it be the design of Providence to extirpate these savages in order to make room for cultivators of the earth, it seems not improbable that rum may be the appointed means."[36]

Failing, however, to convince society that drugs were the root cause of all societal problems, the Reagan/Bush administrations shifted their attention to another enemy: terrorism. According to Edward Said, a noted scholar and professor at Columbia University:

The search for a post-Soviet foreign devil has come to rest . . . on Islam. . . . Never mind that most Islamic countries today are too poverty-stricken, tyrannical, and hopelessly inept militarily as well as scientifically to be much of a threat to anyone except their own citizens; and never mind that the most powerful of them—like Saudi Arabia, Egypt, Jordan, and Pakistan—are totally within the U.S. orbit. What matters to "experts" like [Judith] Miller, Samuel Huntington, Martin Kramer, Bernard Lewis, David Pipes, Steven Emerson, and Barry Rubin, plus a whole battery of Israeli academics, is to make sure that the "threat" is kept before our eyes, the better to excoriate Islam for terror, despotism, and violence, while assuring themselves profitable consultancies, frequent TV appearances and book contracts.[37]

This pattern was evident in the Oklahoma bombing, where over one hundred innocent victims died. After "a law enforcement source said that several factors suggested a link, including the size and sophistication of the bomb and the fact that several militant Middle Eastern groups are based in Oklahoma,"[38] the focus of the initial investigation was mostly on international terrorism, particularly Islamic groups. Interestingly, after Timothy McVeigh and James Nichols, both white Americans, were identified as suspects, the language shifted swiftly from terrorism to militia groups, but the media and the "experts" did not demonize and dehumanize the whole white American culture as they usually do to Arabs. This differential treatment of ethnicities points to the privilege inherent in being white in the U.S. context. The differential treatment was evident in the numerous media analyses of what leads angry white men and militia groups to acts of terrorism. Psychological profiles of McVeigh and other militia members became the focus of media coverage, and militia members (mostly white) were given airtime to explain their position. In the case of international terrorism, particularly terrorism linked to Islamic movements, this does not occur.

It is rare to find the U.S. media discussing how more often than not, terrorism is the work of groups and has its own—if perverse—rationale. Yet this rationale is never mentioned in the discussions of the challenge of terrorism, despite the fact that there is a clear causal connection between U.S. government acts and terrorist retaliation. For example, the United States became a major target of terrorism in the Middle East after the ill-conceived 1982 military mission in Lebanon, which made this country a direct participant in the Arab-Israeli dispute.[39]

With the shift in the national media away from Islamic terrorism, we have been given a lasting enemy: so-called illegal immigration. This enemy was readily seized upon by syndicated columnist Richard Estrada, whose own grandfather immigrated to El Paso, Texas, in 1916. Estrada recently declared that "illegal immigration threatens our national security"[40] substantiating his claim by stating that Americans in Los Angeles cannot find jobs because of immigrants. Therefore, he argued that we need to militarize the border in order to protect the spirit of Proposition 187 and take our country back. Estrada's reference to "taking our country back" means keeping Mexicans from their own land in much the same way as Native Americans have been kept from theirs, for Mexicans inhabited the land until the U.S. government legitimized the expropriation of almost half of Mexico through the Mexican-American War, which it intentionally provoked. This expropriation was justified through the idea that if you fight for it and you win, you deserve the land. The attempt to reduce war for land expropriation is eloquently captured in Carl Sandburg's poem, "The People, Yes":

"Get off this estate."
"What for?"
"Because it's mine."
"Where did you get it?"
"From my father."
"Where did he get it?"
"From his father."
"And where did he get it?"
"He fought for it."
"Well, I'll fight you for it."[41]

If we critically deconstruct our seemingly democratic society, we begin to understand how the ideological construction of ethnicity and race has played an important role in the reproduction and reinscription of undemocratic structures and power relations along racial, ethnic, cultural, class, and linguistic lines. Thus, it is imperative that we describe and analyze the historical and social conditions of the United States in order to understand how this ideology produces and reproduces inequalities through invisible institutional mechanisms. Central to these hidden mechanisms, language has played a pivotal role in the production and reproduction of distorted realities.

Language and the Construction of Racism

Given the sophisticated use of language in the social construction of the "other" in dehumanizing cultural subjects, we feel that educators need to become "cultural brokers" to help create a psychologically beneficial pedagogical space for all students. Educators also need to make sure that they do not teach a form of literacy that gives learners a lasting experience of subordination. We need to understand that language is the only effective tool for us to deconstruct the web of ideological manipulation that makes the white cultural and ethnic group invisible and outside the realm of study.

Educators, particularly those working with multilingual and multicultural students, need to understand how discourses, according to linguist Oliver Reboul, are very often anchored in shock words, terms or expressions produced by themselves [which,] due to their strong connotations, provoke a reaction no matter what sentence within which they are inserted.[42]

In other words, these terms, expressions, and words have a positive association, almost independent of their meanings. For example, in the present discussion of welfare reform, the word "reform" provokes a positive effect that forces most middle-class white individuals to leave its meaning in different contexts, unexamined. Who in the white-dominated middle class would oppose reforming a welfare system they believe only benefits lazy individuals living off of those who work hard to pay taxes? Who in this segment of the middle class would oppose reforming what Patrick Buchanan characterizes as a "social catastrophe" and as "Great Society programs not only [responsible] for financial losses but also for the drop in high school test scores, drug problems and a generation of children and youth with no fathers, no faith and no dreams other than the lure of the streets."[43]

Thus, "welfare reform for the poor" represents a positive shock phrase to the majority of white middle-class individuals, who feel put upon by paying high taxes to, in their view, support lazy individuals who are poor because they do not want to work. When one points out that a higher percentage of their taxes goes to support welfare for the rich, the cry is uniform, immediate, and aggressive: there is no room in the United States for incitement of class warfare. When the call is to reform welfare for the rich, the reaction is as swift as it is disingenuous. By changing the context of welfare reform from the poor to the rich, the shockword impact changes accordingly, from a positive to a negative effect. Let's examine some positions taken by politicians and policymakers with respect to class warfare:

- Alfonse M. D'Amato, Republican senator from New York, set the tone: "There is something that I think is very dangerous taking place in this nation. Let me tell you what it is. It is class warfare under the theory of 'let's get the rich guy, the richest 1 percent.' So we set them up, target them. Those are the people we are going to get."
- William S. Cohen, Republican senator from Maine, put it this way: "We are talking about taxing the rich. Once again, we are engaging in classic class warfare.
- Bob Dole, former Republican senator from Kansas: "I do not know how long we can continue that kind of class warfare."
- Slade Gordon, Republican senator from Washington: "While reducing the budget deficit may he the most important issue before this Congress, the president and his allies in Congress are offering this country what amounts to class warfare. I object to these higher taxes."
- Robert K. Dornan, former Republican representative from California, said: "To sell this program of higher taxes, Clinton and his liberal allies here in the House have turned to the standard liberal theme of class warfare, though they have couched it in terms of 'progressivity,' 'fairness,' and 'equality.'"
- Jim Bunning, Republican representative from Kentucky, labeled the legislation "a historic class warfare scheme."
- Gerald B. H. Solomon, Republican representative from New York, observed: "As young Russians cover Marx's statue in Moscow with flippant slogans such as 'workers of the world, forgive me,' America is awash in the Marx-Leninesque rhetoric of class warfare."[44]

These politicians are correct in stating that we have ongoing class warfare in the United States, but it is actually warfare on the middle class and the poor, not on the rich, as they claim. Since the early 1960s, there has been a progressive change in the tax code that enriches the upper class while eroding the economic base of the middle and lower classes.[45] This transfer of wealth from the poor and middle classes to the upper class has created an enormous gap between a small elite and a growing sea of poverty. For example, 2 percent of the U.S. upper class controls 48 percent of the nation's wealth, while 51 percent of African-American children live in poverty.[46] Upon close examination of organizations benefiting from the present tax code, we soon realize how the policymakers have insistently waged class warfare that benefits large corporations. For example:

- The Chase Manhattan Corporation, based in New York, is the parent company of Chase Manhattan Bank, the global banking institution. For the years 1991 and 1992, Chase reported income before taxes of $1.5 billion. The company paid $25 million in income tax, which represents a tax rate of 1.7 percent. The official corporate tax rate in those years was 34 percent.
- The Ogden Corporation, diversified supplier of aviation, building, and waste management services, reported income before taxes of $217 million. The company paid less than $200,000 in taxes. Given that the rate of $1 being paid for every $1,085 earned the Ogden corporation, if this were the case for a working class family of four earning $25,000 a year, they would be proportionally responsible for paying approximately $25 in taxes each year.
- While the very rich corporations paid a minuscule percentage of their reported income in taxes, individuals with incomes between $13,000 and $15,000 paid taxes at a rate of 7.2 percent, or four times the Chase rate.[47]

As we can see, the power of ideology is so insidious that the unanalyzed positive association of shock words such as "welfare reform" is often accepted by the very people who are in a position to be adversely affected by such reform. Thus, many working-class white people are misled by the positive illusion of "welfare reform" without realizing that they themselves are, perhaps, one paycheck away from benefiting from the very social safety net they want reformed or destroyed. In an age of institutional downsizing (which is a euphemism for corporate greed and maximization of profit), the economic stability of both the white middle and working classes is fast disappearing, thus creating an even more urgent need to make horizontal the economic oppression that is eating away their once more or less secure economic status. By this, we mean that both the white middle and working classes need a scapegoat in order to blame the "other" for their present economic insecurities.

Unfortunately, the same ideology that anchors its discourse on the positive effect of shock words also prevents us from having access to the subtext containing the opposite meaning of the illusory "reality." It is for this reason that conservative politicians who propose welfare reform as a panacea for all the economic ills of our society will not tolerate a counterresponse that challenges the false assumption that welfare recipients are the cause of the nation's economic problems. For welfare reform to be equally exercised, it would have to include welfare reform for the rich, who are most responsible for exacerbating the already huge gap between themselves and the poor. Since discussion concerning welfare reform for the rich is beyond question, the only way to rationalize support for welfare reform is to stay at the level of the positive effect of the shock word that often obfuscates the reality.

As stated earlier, shock words, terms, and expressions do not produce only positive effects. According to Oliver Reboul, they can also "produce by themselves negative effects that disqualify those who use these shock words."[48] Thus, the use of terms such as "welfare for the rich," "oppression," "radical," and "activist" often provokes a negative effect that prevents a thorough analysis of the reality encoded by these terms. In other words, if the word "oppression" is not allowed as part of the debate, there will be no need to identify the "oppressor." An example of this occurred when author Macedo asked a colleague whom he considered politically progressive to read a manuscript of a book he was coauthoring with Paulo Freire. She asked him, a bit irritably, "Why do you and Paulo insist on using this Marxist jargon? Many readers who may enjoy reading Paulo may be put off by the jargon." Macedo calmly explained to her that the equation of Marxism with jargon did not fully capture the richness of Freire's analysis. In fact, his language was the only means through which he could do justice to the complexity of the various concepts dealing with oppression. Macedo asked his colleague to imagine that instead of writing *The*

Pedagogy of the Oppressed, Freire had written *The Pedagogy of the Disenfranchised.* The first title utilizes a discourse that conveys the fact that there is an active agent of oppression, whereas the second fails to do so. If there are oppressed, there must be oppressors. What would be the counterpart of disenfranchised? The pedagogy of the disenfranchised dislodges the agent of the action, leaving in doubt who bears the responsibility for such actions. This leaves the door wide open for blaming victims for their own disenfranchisement. This example is a clear case in which the object of oppression can be also understood as the subject of oppression. Such language distorts reality. Thus, it is not surprising that most people prefer a discourse of euphemism based on shock words that do not name it.

The dominant discourse uses the presence of taboo words such as "class" and "oppression" to dismiss a counter-discourse that challenges the falsification of reality. Thus, to call for welfare reform for the rich is immediately dismissed as "class warfare," a taboo concept not in keeping with the myths that the United States is a classless society. In fact, the ideological power of this myth is so strong that policymakers, the media, and educators can refer to the "working class" being pressured by foreign imports or a "middle class" overburdened by taxes, while simultaneously denying the existence of class differences in the United States. If in fact we live in a classless society, why do we constantly refer to the existence of the working class versus the middle class? What is omitted from the dominant discourse is the existence of the term upper class." As a substitute, the dominant discourse creates euphemisms such as "rich," "well-to-do," and "affluent." By closing the link between the working, middle, and upper classes, it would be impossible to sustain the myth that we live in a classless society. Therefore, it is important that the dominant discourse suppress the term "upper class" and, in so doing, deny its existence.

By forbidding the use of the term "upper class," the dominant discourse prevents the public from gaining an understanding of the mechanisms used as obstacles to the development of spaces for dialectal relationships. For example, "radicalism" is a shock word that triggers a negative effect. Those involved in work that is considered by the dominant discourse as "radical" are dismissed as political, and therefore not scientific, and are often prevented from taking part in discussions, particularly if a particular agenda is to maintain the status quo. Similarly, denouncing racism with strong conviction is often considered radical. A preferred position is to acknowledge that racism exists but not to advocate doing anything about it, thus not challenging the very structures that produce racism. In fact, to denounce racism with conviction becomes a worse social crime than the racist acts themselves. In the political sphere, politicians use taboo words to effectively control the population, manufacture consent, and dismiss any challenge presented by a counter-discourse. Other taboo shock words such as "socialism," "communism," and "Marxism" have the same effect and are often successfully used for ideological control.

Consider the negative effect of the shock word "migrant." Why do we designate Latinos who migrate to other geographical areas to seek better economic opportunities as "migrants" and, in contrast, call the English migrants who came to Plymouth, Massachusetts, "settlers"? And why do we continue to call the Hispanic community of migrant workers that has been here for centuries "migrant" yet fail to use the same term to categorize the large migration of Massachusetts workers to Florida and elsewhere during the last recession. Clearly, the term is not used to describe the migration of groups of people moving from place to place but to label and typecast certain Hispanics ethnically and racially, while using this typecast to denigrate and devalue the Hispanic culture. "Migrant" not only relegates the Hispanics labeled as such to a lower status in our society, but it also robs them of their citizenship as human beings who participate and contribute immensely to our society. The following poem was distributed to Republican legislators in California by State Assemblyman William Knight:

Ode to the New California

I come for visit, get treated regal,
So I stay, who care illegal.

Cross the border poor and broke,

Take the bus, see customs bloke.

Welfare say come down no more,
We send cash right to your door.

Welfare checks they make you wealthy,
Medi-Cal it keep you healthy.

By and by, I got plenty money,
Thanks, American working dummy.

Write to friends in mother land,
Tell them come as fast as can.

They come in rags and Chebby trucks,
I buy big house with welfare bucks.

Fourteen families all move in,
Neighbor's patience growing thin.

Finally, white guy moves away,
I buy his house and then I say,

Send for family, they just trash,
But they draw more welfare cash.

Everything is much good,
Soon we own the neighborhood.

We have hobby, it's called "breeding,"
Welfare pay for baby feeding.

Kids need dentist? Wife need pills?
We get free, we got no bills.

We think America damn good place,

Too damn good for white man's race.

If they no like us, they can go,
Got lots of room in Mexico.[49]

When the legislator's Latino caucus complained that the poem was
racist, Knight explained without apologizing that he thought the poem
was "clever" and "funny,"[50] adding that it was not intended to offend
anyone.

In the United States, how can we honestly speak of human freedom in a society that generates and yet ignores ghettos, reservations,
human misery, and savage inequalities, and then have the audacity to
joke about it? How can we honestly speak of human freedom when
the state of California passes Proposition 187, which robs millions of
children of their human citizenship? The law proposes to:

1. refuse citizenship to children born on U.S. soil to illegal parents
2. end the legal requirement that the state provide emergency
   health care to illegal immigrants
3. deny public education to children of illegal immigrants, and
4. create tamperproof identification cards for legal immigrants so
   they can receive benefits.[51]

What becomes clear through our discussion is that our "democracy" remains paralyzed by a historical legacy that has bequeathed to
us rampant social inequality along the lines of ethnicity and race.

Conclusion: A Pedagogy of Hope

As cultural brokers, we must have the courage and ethical integrity to
denounce any and all attempts to actively dehumanize the very students from whom we make our living as teachers. We need to have
the courage and ethical integrity to say to Patrick Buchanan, John Silber, Pete Wilson, and President Clinton that no human being is illegal, much less alien. Rather than the "all-out cultural war" called for
by Buchanan, what we need is cultural peace. The real challenge for

educators is how schools can be brokers in this peace process, or, in other words, how educators can forge cultural unity through diversity.

We conclude by proposing a pedagogy of hope that is informed by tolerance, respect, and solidarity. A pedagogy that rejects the social construction of images that dehumanize the "other"; a pedagogy that points out that in our construction of the other we become intimately tied with that other; a pedagogy that teaches us that by dehumanizing the other we become dehumanized ourselves. In short, we need a pedagogy of hope that guides us toward the critical road of truth, rather than myths and lies, toward reclaiming our dignity and our humanity. A pedagogy of hope will point us toward a world that is more harmonious and more humane, less discriminatory, less dehumanizing, and more just. A pedagogy of hope will reject Patrick Buchanan's and John Silber's policies of hatred, bigotry, and division while celebrating diversity within unity. In other words, a pedagogy of hope points to "[the] path through which men and women can become conscious about their presence in the world. The way they act and think when they develop all their capacities, taking into consideration their needs, but also the needs and aspirations of others."[52]

A pedagogy of hope will teach us that the social construction of otherness, in its ideological makeup, constitutes the raison d'être for aggression or the rationalization of aggression. In creating the social and cultural separateness that demonizes so-called illegals, for example, the dominant group creates a distance from them that engenders in the dominant groups an ignorance that borders on stupidification.[53] By creating rigid borders, either by building or maintaining walls between people or nations, we inevitably end up with the same reality where things lose their fluidity while generating more tensions and conflicts.[54]

The creation of otherness not only fosters more ignorance on the part of those in power, but also fails to provide the dominant group with the necessary tools to empathize with the demonized other. The dominant group loses its humanity in its inability to feel bad for discriminating against other human beings. The dominant group's ability to demonize and its inability to empathize with the other points to the inherent demon in those who dehumanize.

A pedagogy of hope will also point out to President Clinton and others that they could learn a great deal from those human beings who, by virtue of their place of birth, race, or ethnicity, have been reduced to the non-status of aliens. As Carlos Fuentes has written: "People and their cultures perish in isolation, but they are born or reborn in contact with other men and women, with men and women of another culture, another creed, another race. If we do not recognize our humanity in others, we shall not recognize it in ourselves."[55]

In order to fully embrace a humanizing pedagogy, we must go beyond technicism in classroom instruction and engage other fundamental knowledge that are seldom taught to us in our preparation as teachers. This knowledge includes, according to Paulo Freire,

> the courage to dare, in the full sense of the term, to speak about love without fear of being called ascientific, if not anti-scientific. It is necessary to say, scientifically and not in a pure bla-bla-bla, that we study, we learn, we teach, we know with our entire body. With feelings, with emotions, with desire, with fear, with doubts, with passion and also with critical reasoning. However, critical reasoning alone is not sufficient. It is necessary to dare so that we never dichotomize cognition from the emotional self. It is necessary to dare so we can remain teaching for a long time under conditions that we all know too well, low pay, lack of respect and resisting the risk of falling into cynicism.[56]

It is necessary to dare, to learn to dare, to say no to the bureaucratization of the mind to which we are exposed daily. It is necessary to dare to say that racism is a curable disease. It is necessary to dare to speak of difference as a value and to say that it is possible to find unity in diversity.

Notes

1. James Baldwin, *The Price of the Ticket: Collected Nonfiction* 1948-1985 (New York: St. Martin's/MAREK), p. 409.
2. Derrick Z. Jackson, "Muted Voices in the Newsroom," *Boston Globe*, September 2, 1993, p. 15.
3. bell hooks, *Talking Back: Thinking Feminist, Thinking Black* (Boston: South End

Press, 1989), p. 22.

4. Pepi Leistyna, "Racenicity: Whitewashing Ethnicity," in ed. Donaldo Macedo *Tongue-Tying Multiculturalism*, (work in progress).

5. Stanley Aronowitz, "Ethnicity and Higher Education in the U.S.," in ed. Donaldo Macedo *Tongue-Typing Multiculturalism* (work in progress).

6. Leistyna, "Racenicity."

7. Michael Rezendes, "Declaring 'Cultural War': Buchanan Opens '96 Run," *Boston Globe*, March 21, 1995, p. 1.

8. Cited in Henry Giroux, *Border Crossings: Cultural Workers and the Politics of Education* (New York: Routledge, 1992), p. 20.

9. Henry A. Giroux, "Transgression of Difference," in *Culture and* Difference: Critical Perspectives on Bicultural Experiences (Westport, CT: Bergin & Garvey, in press).

10. John Fiske, *Power Plays, Power Works* (London: Verso Press, 1994), p. 13.

11. Steven Randall, Jim Naureckus, and Jeff Cohen, *The Way Things Ought to Be: Rush Limbaugh's Reign of Error* (New York: New Press, 1995), pp. 47-54.

12. Randall et al., *The Way Things Ought to Be*, p. 10.

13. Donaldo Macedo, *Literacies of Power: What Americans Are Not Allowed to Know* (Boulder, CO: Westview Press, 1994), p. 10.

14. C. P. Otero, ed., *Language and Politics* (New York: Black Rose Books, 1988), p. 681.

15. Cited in Giroux, *Border Crossings*, p. 230.

16. Adam Pertman, "Buchanan Announces Presidential Candidacy," *Boston Globe*, December 15, 1991, p. 13.

17. William Clinton, "Clinton Speech Envisions Local Empowerment," in *Congressional Quarterly*, January 28, 1995, p. 303.

18. Derrick Jackson, "The Assassination of Affirmative Action," *Boston Globe*, March 22, 1995, p. 13.

19. Ibid.

20. Ibid.

21. bell hooks, Gloria Steinem, Urvashi Vaid, and Naomi Wolf, "Let's Get Real About Feminism: The Backlash, the Myths, the Movement," *Ms.*, September/October 1993, p. 39.

22. Jackson, "The Assassination of Affirmative Action," p. 13.

23. Donaldo P. Macedo, "Literacy for Stupidification: The Pedagogy of Big Lies," *Harvard Educational Review*, 63 (1993), 183-206.

24. Derrick D. Bell, *Faces at the Bottom of the Well: The Permanence of Racism* (New York: Basic Books, 1992), p. xiii.

25. "Horde Invasion," Editorial, *Boston Globe*, January 26, 1990, p. 12.

26. David Nyhan, "David Duke Sent 'em a Scare but Now He Faces the Old Pro," *Boston Globe*, October 24, 1991, p. 13.

27. Ibid.

28. Bill Alex Talk Radio Show, WBET, Brockton, Massachusetts, March 17, 1994.

29. "Trouble on the Mexican Border," *US News and World Report*, April 24, 1995, p. 10.

30. Ibid.

31. David T. Goldberg, *Racist Culture* (Oxford, Eng.: Blackwell, 1993), p. 6.

32. Ibid.

33. Ibid.

34. Peter Applebone, "Goals Unmet, Duke Reveals the Perils in Effort to Increase Black Faculty," *New York Times*, September 19, 1993, p. 1.

35. Adam Pertman, "CIA-Drug Link Stories Outrage Blacks in L. A.," Boston Globe, October 6, 1996, p. 1.

36. Russell B. Nye, ed. *Autobiography and Other Writings by Benjamin Franklin* (Boston: Houghton Mifflin, 1958), pp. 112-113.

37. Edward W. Said, "A Devil Theory of Islam," *The Nation*, August 12/19, 1996, p. 28.

38. Paul Quinn Judge and Charles Seamot, "Specialists Say the Attack Makes Turning Point in US," *Boston Globe*, April 20, 1995, p. 24.

39. Dimitri, K. Simes, "Using Wisdom to Avert Terrorism," *Boston Globe*, August 8, 1996, p. A21.

40. Richard Estrada, "Immigration: Setting the Context," paper presented at "In or Out? Immigration and Proposition 187," conference held at Harvard Graduate School of Education, February 15, 1995.

41. Carl Sandburg, *The People, Yes* (New York: Harcourt, Brace & World, 1964), p. 75.

42. Oliver Reboul, *Lenguage e Ideologia* (Mexico City: Fondo de Cultura Economica, 1986), p. 116.

43. Pertman, "Buchanan Announces Presidential Candidacy," p. 1.

44. Donald I. Bartlett and James B. Steele, *America: Who Really Pays the Taxes?* (New York: Simon & Schuster, 1994), p. 93.

45. Robert Kuttner, "The Rewards of Our Labor Are Increasingly Unequal," *Boston Globe*, September 4, 1995, p. 15.

46. Macedo, *Literacies of Power*, pp. 42-43.

47. Ibid.

48. Reboul, Lenguage e ldeologia, p. 117.

49. From "I Love America!" a poem distributed in May 1995 to California Legislators by State Assemblyman William J. Knight, quoted in Dan Morain and Hank Gladstone, "Racist Verse Stirs Up Anger in Assembly," *Los Angeles Times*, May 19, 1993, p. 3. *The California Journal* 24, no. 7 (1993), pp. 42-43, included the following abstract concerning this poem: GOP Assemblyman Pete Knight of Palmdale, CA distributed a poem to Assembly Republicans in May 1993 that may have been the most offensive sliver of verse publicly distributed by a member inside the confines of the state Capitol since the end of WWII. The distribution of the racist poem about illegal Latino immigrants is discussed."

50. Morain and Gladstone, "Racist Verse Stirs Up Anger in Assembly."

51. Proposition 187 Text approved by California voters on November 8, 1994.

52. Paulo Freire and Frei Betto, *Essa Escola Chamada Vida* (Sao Paulo: Editora Scipione, 1989), p. 32.

53. Macedo, "Literacy for Stupidification," pp. 183-206.

54. Vitor J. Rodrigues, *A Nova Ordem Estupidoldgica* (Lisbon: Livros Horizonte, 1995), p. 18.

55. Carlos Fuentes, "The Mirror of the Other," *The Nation*, March 30, 1992, p. 411.

56. Paulo Freire, *Teachers as Cultural Workers: Letters to Those Who Dare Teach* (Boulder, CO: Westview Press, 1998, p. 3).

CHAPTER 2

TONGUE-TIED MULTICULTURALISM

So, if you want to really hurt me,
talk badly about my language.

—*Gloria Anzaldúa*

In the preceding chapter we began to highlight the importance of language in the construction of human subjectivities. Although the literature in multicultural education correctly stresses the need to valorize and appreciate cultural differences as a process for students to come to voice, the underlying assumption is that the celebration of other cultures will take place in English only, a language that may provide students from other linguistic and cultural backgrounds with the experience of subordination. In this chapter we discuss the issue of language and its role in multicultural education, particularly in the multicultural debate in the United States, where the issue of language is often relegated to a secondary status. In fact, some multiculturalists, without saying so, assume that multicultural education can be effectively implemented through English only. Such an assumption neglects to appreciate how English, as a dominant language, even in a multicultural classroom, may continue to devalue students and speakers of other languages. In other words, one cannot celebrate different cultural values through the very dominant language that devalues, in many ways, the cultural experiences of different cultural groups. Multiculturalists need to understand that language is the only means through which one comes to consciousness. In our chapter we provide a critical analysis of the politics of language and its role in multicultural and multilingual education.

With the exception of a small number of critical multiculturalists such as Christine Sleeter, Henry Giroux, Sonia Nieto, and Peter McLaren, most multicultural educators have simply failed to undertake the necessary critical analysis of the politics of language and its role in multicultural education. The dearth of critical work concerning the ideological construction of language and its cultural manifestation is due, primarily, to two fundamental factors: (1) the teaching of cultural tolerance as an end in itself, and (2) the lack of political clarity in the bilingual education movement, which, in turn, prevented even the most committed educators from understanding the neocolonial language policy that informed and shaped bilingual program developments.

As we argued in the last chapter, there is a preponderance in the field of multicultural education to teach tolerance. This posture is not only paternalistic but it also fails to critique its underlying assumptions so as to understand the power asymmetry that characterizes the constellation of cultures within which we live, particularly in the age of globalization. The emphasis on the teaching of cultural tolerance often fails to denude the privilege inherent in such posture. In other words, promising the "other" a dose of tolerance so we can get along, not only eclipses real opportunities for the development of mutual respect and cultural solidarity but also hides the privilege and paternalism inscribed in the proposition "I will tolerate you even though your culture is repugnant." It is the same paternalism that is often encoded as: "We need to empower minorities" or "we need to give them voice." First of all, we need to become keenly aware that voice is not something to be given by those in power. Voice requires struggle and the understanding of both possibilities and limitations. The most educators can do is to create structures that would enable submerged voices to emerge. It is not a gift. Voice is a human right. It is a democratic right.

The teaching of tolerance that is ushering multicultural education into the twenty-first century has brought with it highly complex and challenging realities that are still ill understood but have enormous ramifications for a more humanized world. Not only has the teaching of a cultural tolerance not dealt with the great economic disparity created by the widening gap between the so-called first and third worlds, but the resulting gulf between the rich and poor countries has manifested itself in unpredictable immigration patterns that have exacerbated our already racist societies. For example, in the last few years, for the first time in human history, over one hundred million people immigrated from one part of the globe to another. With it, this exponential increase in immigration has given rise to a dramatic increase of racism and xenophobia. In France, the ultra-right National Front Party headed by Jean-Marie LePen, has mounted an incessant attack on immigrants, particularly the Muslims from former French colonies. In Germany, there has been a significant increase in the number of neo-Nazi groups who have been responsible for a number of house bombings against the Turks. The Turks, in turn, have remain no less violent against the Kurds as they arbitrarily wiped out hundreds of villages, sentencing the Kurds to a life of half-citizenry in the margins of ghetto existence. In Austria, Russia, and some Scandinavian countries, the level of anti-Semitism is also on the rise. Similar levels of xenophobia have been attested in Spain, particularly against North African immigrants and Gypsies.

Against a landscape of increased globalized racism and xenophobia, we doubt very much that the teaching of tolerance alone will enable us to critically understand how capitalist forces construct, shape, and maintain the cruel reality of racism. We also doubt that the teaching of tolerance could equip educators with the necessary critical tools to understand how language is often used to ideologically construct realities that veil the raw racism that devalues, disconfirms, and poisons other cultural identities. Even within the bilingual education movement, most educators failed to understand the neocolonialist ideology that informs the bilingual debate to the extent that they structured their arguments within a reductionistic view of language.

If we analyze closely the ideology that informs and shapes the present debate over bilingual education and the present polemic over the primacy of Western heritage versus multiculturalism, we can begin to see and understand that the ideological principles that sustain those debates are consonant with the structures and mechanisms of a colonial ideology designed to devalue the cultural capital and values of the colonized.

It is only through a full understanding of our colonial legacy that we can begin to comprehend the complexity of our bilingualism in the United States. For most linguistic minority speakers in the United States, their bilingualism is not characterized by the ability to speak two languages. There is a radical difference between a dominant speaker learning a second language and a minority speaker acquiring the dominant language. While the former involves the addition of a second language to one's linguistic repertoire, the latter usually provides the minority speaker with the experience of subordination in speaking both his or her language, which is devalued by the dominant values, and the dominant language that he or she has learned, often under coercive conditions. Both the colonized context and the asymmetrical power relations with respect to language use in the United States create, on the one hand, a form of forced bilingualism and, on the other, what Albert Memmi appropriately calls a linguistic drama:

> In the colonial context, bilingualism is necessary. It is a condition for all culture, all communication and all progress. But while the colonial bilinguist is saved from being walled in, he suffers a cultural catastrophe which is never completely overcome.
>
> The difference between native language and cultural language is not peculiar to the colonized, but colonial bilingualism cannot be compared to just any linguistic dualism. Possession of two languages is not merely a matter of having two tools, but actually means participation in two physical and cultural realms. Here, the two worlds symbolized and conveyed by the two tongues are in conflict; they are those of the colonizer and the colonized.
>
> Furthermore, the colonized's mother tongue, that which is sustained by his feelings, emotions, and dreams, that in which his tenderness and wonder are expressed, thus that which holds the greatest emotional impact, is precisely the one which is the least valued. It has no stature in the country or in the concept of peoples. If he wants to obtain a job, make a place for himself, exist in the community and the world, he must first bow to the language of his masters. In the linguistic conflict within the col-

onized, his mother tongue is that which is crushed. He himself sets about discarding this infirm language, hiding it from the sight of strangers. In short, colonial bilingualism is neither a purely bilingual situation, in which an indigenous tongue coexists with a purist's language (both belonging to the same world of feeling), nor a simple polyglot richness benefiting from an extra but relatively neuter alphabet; it is a linguistic drama.[1]

An example par excellence concerning how our society treats different forms of bilingualism is reflected in our tolerance toward certain types of bilingualism and lack of tolerance toward other bilingualism expressions. Most of us have tolerated various degrees of bilingualism on the part of foreign language teachers and professors that range from heavy English accent to serious deficiency in the mastery of the foreign language they teach. Nevertheless, these teachers, with rare exceptions, have been granted tenure, have been promoted within the institutions where they teach and, in some cases, have become "experts" and "spokespersons" for various cultural and linguistic groups in our communities. On the other hand, if bilingual teachers are speakers of a subordinated language who speak English as a second language with an accent, the same level of tolerance is not accorded to them. Take the case of Westfield, Massachusetts, when "about 400 people there signed a petition asking state and local officials to ban the hiring of any elementary teacher who speaks English with an accent,"[2] because according to them, "accents are catching."[3] The petition was in response to the hiring of a Puerto Rican teacher assigned to teach in the system. As you can readily see, empirical studies that neglect to fully investigate this linguistic drama and treat bilingualism as mere communication in two languages invariably end up reproducing those ideological elements characteristic of the communication between colonizer and colonized.

English only as a Form of Colonialism

While conservative educators have been very vocal in their attempt to abolish bilingual education due to, according to them, its lack of academic success, these same educators have conspicuously remained silent about the well-documented failure of foreign language educa- tion. In spite of the general failure of foreign language education in the United States, no one is advocating closing down foreign language departments in schools. Paradoxically, the same educators who pro- pose the dismantling of bilingual education programs that have a higher probability of producing bilingual speakers, reiterate their sup- port for foreign language education with the aim of developing bilin- gualism even though the failure rate of becoming fully bilingual through foreign language education is exponentially greater than in bilingual programs.

The English Only movement's position points to a pedagogy of exclusion that views the learning of English as education itself. What its proponents fail to question is under what conditions English will be taught and by whom. For example, insisting on immersing non- English speaking students in English as a Second Language (ESL) programs taught by untrained music, art, and social sciences grand- fathered teachers (as is the case in Massachusetts with the grandfa- ther clause in ESL Certification, will do very little to accomplish the very goal of the English-Only movement. In addition, the proponents of English Only also fail to raise two fundamental questions. First, if English is the most effective educational language, how can we explain that over 60 million Americans are illiterate or functionally illiterate? Second, if education in "English Only" can guarantee lin- guistic minorities a better future, as educators like William Benett promise, why do the majority of black Americans, whose ancestors have been speaking English over 200 years, find themselves still rele- gated to the ghettos?

We want to argue in this chapter that the answer to these questions has nothing to do with whether English is a more viable language of instruction or whether it promises non-English-speaking students full participation both in school and the society at large. This position would point to an assumption that English is, in fact, a superior lan- guage and that we live in a classless, race-blind society. We want to propose that the attempt to institute proper and effective methods of educating non-English-speaking students cannot be reduced simply to issues of language but rests on a full understanding of the ideological elements that generate and sustain linguistic, cultural, and racial discrimination, which represent, in our view, vestiges of a colonial legacy in our democracy.

Many educators will object to the term "colonialism" to characterize the present attack on bilingual education by conservative as well as many liberal educators. Some liberals will go to great length to oppose our characterization of the attack on bilingual education as a form of colonialism, rationalizing that most educators who do not support bilingual education are just ignorant and need to be educated. This is tantamount to saying that racists do not really hate people of color; they are just ignorant. While one cannot argue that they are ignorant, one has to realize that ignorance is never innocent and is always shaped by a particular ideological predisposition. On another level, the attack on bilingual education or a racist act due to ignorance does not make the victims of these acts feel any better about their victimization.

The apologetic stance of some liberals concerning the so-called ignorance on the part of those educators who blindly oppose bilingual education is not surprising, since classical liberalism, as a school of thought and as ideology, always prioritizes the right to private property while relegating human freedom and other rights to mere "epiphenomena or derivatives."[4] A rigorous analysis of thinkers such as Thomas Hobbes and John Locke will clearly show that the real essence of liberalism is the right to own property. The right to private property could only be preserved through self-conservation. This led Liubomir Tadic to pose the following question: "Isn't conservatism a more determinant characteristic for liberalism than the tendency toward freedom?"[5] He concluded that owing to this insip ambiguity, liberalism is always positioned ideologically between revolution and reactionaryism. In other words, liberalism vacillates between two opposing poles.

It is this liberal position of vacillation that, on the one hand, propels many liberals to support bilingual education and, on the other hand, object to the linkage between the attack on bilingual education and colonial language policies.

Any colonized person who experiences firsthand the d
language policies of colonialism can readily see many s
between the colonial ideology and the dominant values that in
U.S. English Only movement. Colonialism imposes "distinction"
ideological yardstick against which all other cultural values are me
ured, including language. On the one hand, this ideological yardstick
serves to overcelebrate the dominant group's language to a level of
mystification (i.e., viewing English as education itself and measuring
the success of bilingual programs only in terms of success in English
acquisition), and, on the other hand, it devalues other languages spoken by an ever-increasing number of students who now populate most
urban public schools. The position of U.S. English Only proponents is
not very different from the Portuguese colonialism that tried to eradicate the use of African languages in institutional life and by inculcating
Africans through the educational system in Portuguese only with
myths and beliefs concerning the savage nature of their cultures.

If we analyze closely the ideology that informs the present debate
over bilingual education—spearheaded by the conservative U.S. English Only movement—and the present polemic over Western heritage
versus multiculturalism, we can begin to see and understand that the
ideological principles that sustain those debates are consonant with
the structures and mechanisms of a colonial ideology as succinctly
described below:

> Culturally, colonialism has adopted a negation to the [native cul-
> ture's] symbolic systems [including the native language], forget-
> ting or undervaluing them even when they manifest themselves
> in action. This way, the eradication of past and the idealization
> and the desire to relive the cultural heritage of colonial societies
> constitute a situation and a system of ideas along with other ele-
> ments situate the colonial society as a class.[6]

If it were not for the colonial legacy, how could we explain the U. S.
educational policies in the Philippines and Puerto Rico. English was
imposed as the only language of instruction in the Philippines while
the imposed American textbook presented the American culture as

...model par excellence for the Philippine
...ation was so prevalent it led T. H. Pardo
...or of the U.S. colonialism, to write the
...glas MacArthur:

...shed all our efforts will be directed to
...selves, to cause a knowledge of the English
...extended and generalized in the Philippines, in
...ough its agency we may adopt its principles, its
...toms, and its peculiar civilization that our redemp-
...on may be complete and radical.[8]

It is the same complete and radical redemption that the United States hoped to achieve in Puerto Rico when Theodore Roosevelt's Commissioner of Education in Puerto Rico, Rolland P. Faulkner, mandated in 1905 that instruction in public schools must be conducted in English, making Puerto Rican schools "agencies of Americanization in the entire country, and where [schools] would present the American ideal to our youth. Children born under the American flag and the American soil should have constantly present this ideal, so that they can feel proud of their citizenship and have the flag that represents the true symbol of liberty. . . ."[9]

By leaving our colonial legacy unexamined, the choice to choose an effective methodology where students are denied the freedom to study their language and culture is, for all practical purposes, a choiceless choice. Instead of becoming enslaved by the management discourse of the present bilingual educational reform that enhances the economic interests of the reformers, while securing their privileged social and cultural positions, educators need to reconnect with our historical past so as to understand the colonial legacy that undermines our democratic aspirations.

Scientism as Neocolonialism

Oppressive dominant ideologies have throughout history resorted to science as a mechanism to rationalize crimes against humanity that range from slavery to genocide by targeting race and other ethnic and cultural traits as markers that license all forms of dehumanization. If we did not suffer from historical amnesia, we would easily understand the ideology that informed Hans Eysenck's psychological proposal, which suggests that "there might be a partly genetic reason for the differences in IQ between black and white people."[10] It is the same historical amnesia that veils dangerous memories, keeping us disconnected from Arthur Jensen's racist proposals published decades ago by the *Harvard Educational Review*.

One could argue that the above cited incidents belong to the dusty archives of earlier generations, but we do not believe we have learned a great deal from historically dangerous memories, considering our society's almost total embrace of scientism as characterized by the success of *The Bell Curve*, by Charles Murray and the former Harvard professor Richard J. Hernstein. It is the same blind acceptance of "naïve" empiricism that is providing fuel to the U.S.-English-Only movement as it attempts to ban bilingual education in the United States. Ironically, when empirical data are provided to demonstrate that bilingual education is an effective approach to educate non-English-speaking students as amply demonstrated by researchers such as Zeynep Beykont, Virginia Collier, Kenji Hakuta, David Ramirez, and Jim Cummins, among others,[11] the data are either ignored or buried in endless debate over research design and are often missing a fundamental point: the inequities that inform and shape most bilingual programs.

By and large the present debate over bilingual education is informed by the positivistic and management models that hide their ideologies in the false call for objectivity, hard data, and scientific rigor; This can be seen, for example, in the comments of Pepi Leistyna's term paper on the political nature of bilingual education by a Harvard professor: "These are unsupported politically motivated claims! [the professor called for] a more linguistic analysis."[12] As Leistyna recounts, this same professor told him: "I hope you have been reading some hard science." The false call for hard science in the social sciences represents a process through which "naïve" empiricists hide their anti-intellectual posture—a posture that is manifested either through censorship of certain bodies of knowledge or through the disarticulation between theories of the discipline and the empirically driven and self-contained studies that enables the pseudoscientists to

> not challenge the territorialization of university intellectual activity or in any way risk undermining the status and core beliefs of their fields. The difference, [for scientists,] is that this blindness or reluctance often contradicts the intellectual imperatives of the very theories they espouse. Indeed, only a theorized discipline can be an effective site for general social critique— that is, a discipline actively engaged in self-criticism, a discipline that is a locus for struggle, a discipline that renews and revises its awareness of its history, a discipline that inquires into its differential relations with other academic fields, and a discipline that examines its place in the social formation and is willing to adapt its writing practices to suit different social functions.[13]

As these theoretical requirements make abundantly clear, Pepi Leistyna's professor's arrogant dismissal of Freire's social critical theories unveil the ideology behind the prescription that Leistyna should have been "reading some hard science." The censorship of political analysis in the current debate over bilingual education exposes the almost illusory and schizophrenic educational practice in which "the object of interpretation and the content of the interpretive discourse are considered appropriate subjects for discussion and scrutiny, but the interests of the interpreter and the discipline and society he or she serves are not."[14]

The disarticulation between the interpretive discourse and the interests of the interpreter is often hidden in the false call for an objectivity that denies the dialectal relationship between subjectivity and objectivity. The false call for objectivity is deeply ingrained in a positivistic method of inquiry. In effect, this has resulted in an epistemological stance in which scientism and methodological refinement are celebrated while "theory and knowledge are subordinated to the imperatives of efficiency and technical mastery, and history is reduced to a minor footnote in the priorities of "empirical" scientific inquiry.[15]

The blind celebration of empiricism has created a culture in which pseudoscientists, particularly in schools of education, who engage in a form of "naive empiricism," believe "that facts are not human statements about the world but aspects of the world itself,"[16] According to Michael Schudson:

> This view was insensitive to the ways in which the "world" is something people construct by the active play of their minds and by their acceptance of conventional—not necessarily "true"—ways of seeing and talking. Philosophy, the history of science, psychoanalysis, and the social sciences have taken great pains to demonstrate that human beings are cultural animals who know and see and hear the world through socially constructed filters.[17]

The socially constructed filters were evident when California voters passed a referendum banning bilingual education. While the school administrators and politicians were gearing up to disband bilingual programs, data from both the San Francisco and San José school systems showed that bilingual graduates were outperforming their English-speaking counterparts.[18] This revelation was met by total silence by the media, the proponents of English Only, and political pundits. This is where the call for objectivity and scientific rigor is subverted by the weight of its own ideology.

What these educators do not realize is that there is a large body of critical litearature that interrogates the very nature of what they consider research. Critical writers such as Donna Haraway,[19] Linda Brodkey, Roger Fowler, Greg Myers among others have painstakingly demonstrated the erroneous claim of "scientific" objectivity that permeates all forms of empirical work in the social sciences. According to Linda Brodkey, "scientific objectivity has too often and for too long been used as an excuse to ignore a social and hence, political practice in which women and people of color, among others, are dismissed as legitimate subjects of research."[20] The blind belief in objectivity not only provides pdeudoscientists with a safe heaven from which they can attempt to prevent the emergence of counterdiscourses that interrogate "the hegemony of positivism and empiricism,[21] but it is also a practice that generates a form of folk theory concerning objectivity believed only by nonscientists. In other words, as Linda Brodkey would so eloquently put it, "any and all knowledge, including that arrived at empirically, is necessarily partial, that is, both an incomplete and an interested account of whatever is envisioned.[22] In fact, what these pseudoscientists consider research, that is, work based on quantitative evaluation results, can never escape the social construction that generated these models of analysis from which the theoretical concepts are always shaped by the pragmatics of the society that devised these evaluation models in the first place.[23] That is, if the results are presented as facts that were originally determined by a particular ideology, these facts cannot in themselves illuminate issues that lie outside of the ideological construction of these facts to begin with.[24] We would warn educators that these evaluation models can provide answers that are correct and nevertheless without truth. A study that concludes that African-American students perform way below white mainstream students in reading is correct, but such a conclusion tells us very little about the material conditions with which African-American students work in the struggle against racism, educational tracking, and the systematic negation and devaluation of their histories. We would propose that the correct conclusion rests in a full understanding of the ideological elements that generate and sustain the cruel reality of racism and economic oppression. Thus an empirical study will produce conclusions without truth if it is disarticulated from the sociocultural reality within which the subjects of the study are situated. For example, an empirical study designed to assess reading achievement of children who live in squalid conditions must factor in the reality faced by these children as accurately described by Jonathan Kozol:

> Crack-cocaine addiction and the intravenous use of heroin, which children I have met here call "the needle drug," are woven into the texture of existence in Mott Haven. Nearly 4,000 heroin injectors, many of whom are HIV-infected, live here. Virtually every child at St. Ann's knows someone, a relative or

neighbor, who has died of AIDS, and most children here know many others who are dying now of the disease. One quarter of the women of Mott Haven who are tested in obstetric wards are positive for HIV. Rates of pediatric AIDS, therefore, are high.

Depression is common among children in Mott Haven. Many cry a great deal but cannot explain exactly why.

Fear and anxiety are common. Many cannot sleep.

Asthma is the most common illness among children here. Many have to struggle to take in a good deep breath. Some mothers keep oxygen tanks, which children describe as "breathing machines," next to their children's beds.

The houses in which these children live, two thirds of which are owned by the City of New York, are often as squalid as the houses of the poorest children I have visited in rural Mississippi, but there is none of the greenness and the healing sweetness of the Mississippi countryside outside their windows, which are often barred and bolted as protection against thieves.[25]

An empirical study that neglects to incorporate in its design the cruel reality just described (and this is often the case in our supposedly classless society) will never be able to fully explain the reasons behind the poor performance of these children. While pseudoscientists will go to great lengths to prevent their research methodologies from being contaminated by the social ugliness described by Kozol in order that they might safeguard their "objectivity" in, say, their study of underachievement of children who live in ghettos, the residents of these ghettos have little difficulty understanding the root causes of their misery as described by a resident of the community named Maria:

If you weave enough bad things into the fibers of a person's life—sickness and filth, old mattresses and other junk thrown in the streets and ugly ruined things, and ruined people, a prison here, sewage there, drug dealers here, the homeless people over there—then give us the very worst schools anyone could think of, hospitals that keep you waiting for ten hours, police that don't show up when someone's dying . . . you can guess that life will not be very nice and children will not have much sense of being glad of who they are. Sometimes it feels like we have been buried six feet under their perceptions. This is what I feel they have accomplished.[26]

What this woman Maria would probably say to researchers is that we do not need another doctoral dissertation to state what is so obvious to the people sentenced to live in this form of human misery. In other words, by locking children in material conditions that are oppressive and dehumanizing we are invariably guaranteeing that they will be academically underachievers. Once the underachievement is guaranteed by these oppressive conditions, it is then very easy for research studies like those described in the *The Bell Curve* by Richard J. Hernstein and Charles Murray, which, in the name of objectivity, are disarticulated from the political and social reality that shaped and maintain these oppressive conditions, to conclude that blacks are genetically wired to be intellectually inferior to whites. Along the same lines, an empirical study that concludes that children who engage in dinner conversation with their parents and siblings achieve higher rates of success in reading is not only academically dishonest but also misleading to the degree that it ignores the class and economic assumptions that all children are guaranteed daily dinners in the company of their parents and other siblings. What generalizations can such a study make about the 12 million children who go hungry every day in the United States? What can a study of this type say to thousands upon thousands of children who are homeless, who do not have a table, and who sometimes do not have food to put on the table that they do not have? A study that makes such sweeping and distorted generalizations about the role of dinner conversations in reading achievement says little about children whose houses are without heat in the winter, and reach dangerously cold conditions that led a father of four children to remark: "You just cover up . . . and hope you wake up the next morning." If the father really believes the study results, he will suggest to his children, after they've all made it through another freezing night alive, that they should have a conversation during dinner the next night, since it will be helpful in their reading development should they be lucky enough to make it through another night alive. What dinner conversation would the Haitian immigrant, Abner Louima, have with his children after being brutally sodomized with a toilet plunger by two white policemen in a New York police precinct? Would his children's reading teacher include as part of his or her literacy development the savage acts committed by the white New York police against their father?

These questions make it clear how distorted empirical study results can be when they are disconnected from the sociocultural reality that informs such studies to begin with. In addition, such distortion feeds into the development of stereotypes that, on the one hand, blame the victims for their own social misery and, on the other hand, rationalize the genetic inferiority hypotheses that are advanced by such pseudoscholars as Murray and Hernstein.[27] What empirical studies often neglect to point out is how easily statistics can be manipulated to take away the human faces of the subjects of study through a process that not only dehumanizes but also distorts and falsifies the reality.

What needs to be fully understood is that educators cannot isolate phoneme-grapheme awareness from social class and cultural identity factors that ultimately shape such awareness.

Fracturing Cultural Identities

Most conservative educators as well as many liberals conveniently embrace a form of "naïve" empiricism in which scientism and methodological refinement are celebrated, issues of equity, class, cultural identity, among other sociocultural knowledges, "are subordinated to the imperatives of efficiency and technical mastery, and [sociocultural factors] are reduced to a minor footnote in the priorities of 'empirical' scientific inquiry."[28] While the fields of bilingual education and English as a Second Language have produced a barrage of studies aimed primarily to demonstrate the effectiveness of English acquisition, these research studies conspicuously fail to raise other fundamental questions: Does cultural subordination affect academic achievement? What is the correlation of social segregation and school success? What role does cultural identity among subordinated students play in linguistic resistance? Does the devaluation of students' culture and language affect reading achievement? Is class a factor in bilingual education? Do material conditions that foster human misery adversely affect academic development?

These questions are rarely incorporated in "naïve" empirical studies that parade under the mantra of scientific "objectivity" as a process to deny the role of ideology in their work so as to ideologically prevent the development of counterdiscourses that interrogate these studies' major assumptions. As Paulo Freire would point out, when these educators claim a scientific posture, for instance, "[they often] try to 'hide' in what [they] regard as the neutrality of scientific pursuits, indifferent to how [their] findings are used, even uninterested in considering for whom or for what interests [they] are working."[29] Because most educators, particularly in schools of education, do not conduct research in "hard sciences," they uncritically attempt to adopt the "neutrality" posture in their work in the social sciences, leaving out the necessary built-in criticism, skepticism, and rigor of hard sciences. In fact, science cannot evolve without a healthy dose of self-criticism, skepticism, and contestation. However, for instance, a discourse of critique and contestation is often viewed as contaminating "objectivity" in social sciences and education. As Freire would argue, these educators "might treat [the] society under study as though [they] are not participants in it. In [their] celebrated impartiality, [they] might approach this real world as if [they] wear 'gloves and masks' in order not to contaminate or be contaminated by it."[30]

The metaphorical "gloves and masks" represent an ideological fog that enables educators to comfortably fragment bodies of knowledge so they can conduct their research, for example, among children who live in Mott Haven to determine their phoneme-grapheme awareness disarticulated from the material conditions of Mott Haven as described by Jonathan Kozol in which children are lock in a chain of oppressive and dehumanizing circumstances that invariably guarantee that they will be academically underachievers.

By reducing the reading principles or the acquisition of English, for instance to pure technicism (i.e., phoneme-grapheme awareness), these educators can easily disarticulate a particular form of knowledge from other bodies of knowledge, thus preventing the interrelation of information necessary to gain a more critical reading of the reality. These metaphorical "gloves and masks" enable educators to engage in a social construction of not seeing that allows them to willfully not understand that behind the empirical data there are always human faces with fractured identities, dreams, and aspirations. The fracturing of cultural identity usually leaves an indelible psychological scar experienced even by those subordinated people who seemingly have "made it" in spite of all forms of oppression. This psychological scar is painfully relived by Gloria Anzaldúa:

"El Anglo," she writes, "con cara de inocente nos arrancó la lengua" [The Anglo with the innocent face has yanked our tongue[31]], and thus sentenced colonized cultural beings to a silenced culture: "Ahogados, escupimos el oscuro. Peleando con nuestra propia sombra el silencio nos sepulta" [Drowned, we spit darkness. Fighting with our very shadow we are buried by silence].[32]

The fragmentation of bodies of knowledge also prevents us from making the necessary linkages so as to understand that the yanking of linguistic minority students' tongues is not only undemocratic but is reminiscent of colonial policies as recounted by the African author Ladislaus Semali:

Then, I went to school, a colonial school, and this harmony was broken. The language of my education was no longer the language of my culture. I first went to Iwa Primary school. Our language of education was not Kiswahili. My struggle began at a very early age constantly trying to find parallels in my culture with what was being taught in the classroom. In school we followed the British colonial syllabus. The books we read in class had been written by Mrs. Bryce, mostly adapted and translated into Kiswahili from British curricula. We read stories and sung songs about having tea in an English garden, taking a ride on the train, sailing in the open seas, and walking the streets of town. These were unfortunately stories far removed from our life experiences. As expected, we memorized them even though they were meaningless.

By the time I was in fifth grade Swahili was no longer the medium of instruction. English had taken over and Kiswahili was only a subject taught once a week. Kichagga was not to be spoken at any time and if caught speaking we were severely punished. Thus, one of the most humiliating experiences was to be caught speaking Kichagga while still in the school grounds. The culprit was given corporal punishment—three to five strokes of the cane on the buttocks.[33]

Expressions like "And then I went to school" are common throughout the world, including First World democracies like the United States where bilingualism and multiculturalism are under a constant assault by the Western cultural commissars. We conveniently fall into historical amnesia by forgetting the English reeducation camps designed primarily to yank Native Americans' tongues. Native American children were taken from their parents and sent to boarding schools with the primary purpose of cutting them off from their "primitive" languages and "savage" cultures. While we ominously forget the dehumanization of American Indian children in the so-called boarding school, we nevertheless proudly denounced the reeducation schools created by communist governments as examples of human rights violation. "And then I went to school" is however, not forgotten by the American Indian writer Joseph H. Suina:

School was a painful experience during those early years. The English language and the new set of values caused me much anxiety and embarrassment. I could not comprehend everything that was happening but yet I could understand very well when I messed up or was not doing well. The negative aspect was communicated too effectively and I became unsure of myself more and more. How I wished I could understand other things as well in school.[34]

Whether we feel the pain of Gloria Anzaldúa's tongue being yanked in our own democracy, whether we connect with the painful experience and embarrassment in American schools as recounted by the Native American author Joseph H. Suina, or whether we listen to the African author Ngugi's lament for the loss of the Gikuyu language in Africa, these experiences undeniably share one common feature: colonization.

We therefore learnt to value words for their meaning and nuances. Language was not a mere string of words. It had a suggestive power well beyond the immediate and lexical meaning. Our appreciation of the suggestive magical power of language was reinforced by the games we played with words through riddles, proverbs, transpositions of syllabes, or through nonsensical but musically arranged words. So we learnt the music of our language on top of the content. The language, through images and symbols, gave us a view of the world, but it had a beauty on its own. The home and the field were then our pre-primary school but what is important for this discussion is that the language of the evening teach-ins and the language of our work in the field were one.

And then I went to school, a colonial, school, and this harmony was broken. The language of my education was no longer the language of my culture.[35]

The reason that even committed educators have failed to understand the linguistic drama that helps shape the cultural identities of most linguistic minority students is they naively treat language as if it were disarticulated from those cultural signposts that are integral for identity formation. As such, the language of minority students became a mere instrument that would facilitate access to both content and English and that could lend itself easily to empirical verification.

However, most of the "naïve" empirical studies in bilingual education cannot but recycle old assumptions and values regarding the meaning and usefulness of the students' native language in education. The notion that education of linguistic minority students is a matter of learning the standard English language still informs the vast majority of bilingual programs and manifests its logic in the renewed emphasis on technical reading and writing skills. For the notion of education of linguistic minority students to become meaningful it has to be situated within a theory of cultural production and viewed as an integral part of the way in which people produce, transform, and reproduce meaning. Bilingual education, in this sense, must be seen as a medium that constitutes and affirms the historical and existential moments of lived culture. Hence, it is an eminently political phenomenon, and must be analyzed within the context of a theory of power relations and an understanding of social and political production and reproduction. By "cultural reproduction" we refer to collective experiences that function in the interest of dominant groups, rather than in the interest of the oppressed groups, that are objects of its policies. Bilingual education programs in the United States have, in fact existed within a de facto neocolonial educational model. We use "cultural production" to refer to specific groups of people producing, mediating, and confirming the mutual ideological elements that merge from and reaffirm their daily lived experiences. In this case, such experiences are rooted in the interest of individual and collective self-determination. It is only through a cultural production model that we can achieve a truly democratic and liberatory educational experience.

While the various debates in the past two decades may differ in their basic assumptions about the education of linguistic minority students, they all share one common feature: they all ignore the role of languages as a major force in the construction of human subjectivities. That is, they ignore the way language may either confirm or deny the life histories and experiences of the people who use it.

The pedagogical and political implications in education programs for linguistic minority students are far-reaching and yet largely ignored. These programs, for example, often contradict a fundamental principle of reading, namely that students learn to read faster and with better comprehension when taught in their native tongue. In addition, the immediate recognition of familiar words and experiences enhances the development of a positive self-concept in children who are somewhat insecure about the status of their language and culture. For this reason, and to be consistent with the plan to construct a democratic society free from vestiges of oppression, a bilingual education program should be based on the rationale that such a program must be rooted in the cultural capital of subordinate groups and have as its point of departure their own language.

Educators must develop radical pedagogical structures that provide students with the opportunity to use their own reality as a basis for literacy. This includes, obviously, the language they bring to the classroom. To do otherwise is to deny linguistic minority students the rights that lie at the core of the notion of a democratic education. The failure to base a literacy program on the minority students' language means that the oppositional forces can neutralize the efforts of educators and political leaders to achieve decolonization of schooling. It is of tantamount importance that the incorporation of the minority language as the primary language of instruction in education of linguistic minority students be given top priority. It is through their own language that linguistic minority students will be able to reconstruct their history and their culture.

We want to emphasize that the minority language has to be understood within the theoretical framework that generates it. Put another way, the ultimate meaning and value of the minority language is not to be found by determining how systematic and rule-governed it is. We know that already. Its real meaning has to be understood through the assumptions that govern it, and it has to be understood via the social, political, and ideological relations to which it points. Generally speaking, the issue of effectiveness and validity often hides the true role of language in the maintenance of the values and interests of the dominant class. In other words, the issue of effectiveness and validity of bilingual education becomes a mask that obfuscates questions about the social, political, and ideological order within which the minority language exists.

In this sense, the students' language is the only means by which they can develop their own voice, a prerequisite to the development of a positive sense of self-worth. As Giroux elegantly states, the student's voice "is the discursive means to make themselves 'heard' and to define themselves as active authors of their worlds.[36] The authorship of one's own world also implies the use of one's own language, and relates to what Mikhail Bakhtin describes as "retelling the story in one's own words."[37] To tell a "story in one's own words" not only represents a threat to those conservative educators who are complicit with dominant ideology but also prevents them from concealing, according to Václav Havel, "their true position and their inglorious modus vivendi, both from the world and from the selves."[38] Simply put, proponents of English Only movement and other educators who are willing to violate linguistic minority students' democratic rights to be educated in their own language as well as in English work primarily to preserve a social (dis)order that according to Jean-Paul Sartre "sanctions misery, chronic hunger, ignorance, or, in general, subhumanity."[39] In essence, educators who refuse to transform the ugliness of human misery, social injustices and inequalities, invariably become educators who, as Sartre so poignantly suggested, "will change nothing and will serve no one, but will succeed only in finding moral confort in malaise."[40]

The Erasure of Class in the Language Debate

By and large the discussion concerning the language of instruction in the bilingual debate is structured in a reductionist binarism of either English or, let's say Spanish. In general, even proponents of bilingual education treat languages as monolithic entities without paying much attention to the multiple varieties spoken by a variety of groups who occupy different class locations in a given society. The assumption is that linguistic minority students speak or should speak the dominant variety of their national language. This position not only ignores far-reaching pedagogical and political implications but it also contradicts a fundamental principle of literacy development, which posits that students learn more effectively when taught in their native language. Thus, in order to be consistent with pedagogical principles that undergird literacy development, educational programs should always be based on the rationale that such a program be rooted in the cultural capital of linguistic minority students and have as its point of departure the linguistic variety spoken by students.

Part of the reason that proponents of bilingual education have neglected to appreciate the worth and the pedagogical value of using the non-standard varieties spoken by most students in bilingual programs is that they neglect to understand the ideology of class that informs their false assumption concerning the standard dominant discourse. Since most students who populate bilingual programs in the United States come from lower classes, the requirement that they perform and assimilate into, let's say, middle- class Spanish (or other national language) academic discourse contradicts the general pedagogical principles that gave rise to bilingual education in the first place. However, to understand the relationship between class and language would require that we move beyond H. T. Wilson's theory that

> In contrast to Europe, America is "open," rendering class theory entirely obsolete. If on the strength of individual achievement anyone can climb the economic and social ladder, structural inequalities may be explained by reference to culture. If the overwhelming majority of Blacks, Asians, and Latinos remained class-locked, this unfortunate circumstance could be ascribed to a culture of poverty, social disorganization, or any explanation that avoids naming the class structure as the chief barrier to economic [success].[41]

The inability to name class structure not only reproduces the false myth that we live in a classless society but it also puts the language of the curriculum beyond question. As a result, for example, the pedagogical and psychological implications of requiring linguistic minority students who speak a variety of their national language to perform in the middle-class academic discourse are far-reaching and yet largely ignored. For instance, to require a student who speaks a chicano Spanish variety to begin his or her literacy in the dominant Spanish academic discourse not only violates the pedagogical principles of bilingual education but it also ignores the psychological consequences of such a requirement, as painfully recounted by Gloria Anzaldúa:

"So, if you want to really hurt me, talk badly about my language. Ethnic identity is twin skin to linguistic identity—I am my language. I cannot take pride of myself until I can accept as legitimate Chicano Texas Spanish, Tex-Mex and all the other languages I speak, I cannot accept the legitimacy of myself. . . . Chicanas who grew up speaking Chicano Spanish have internalized the belief that we speak poor Spanish. It is illegitimate, a bastard language. And because we internalize how our language has been used against us by the dominant culture [English or Spanish], we use our language differences against each other."[42]

By not taking linguistic varieties into account in the development of bilingual programs, we not only risk reproducing the dominant ideology against which we purport to fight, we also fail to demythologize academic discourses so as to develop pedagogical structures that are more relevant and meaningful . In our present discussion academic discourse refers to the middle-class standard and more formal varieties of language that are normally called for in school situations, following Jim Gee's comprehensive definition of discourse as "a socially accepted association among ways of using language, of thinking, and of acting that can be used to identify oneself as a member of a socially meaningful group or 'social network.'"[43] Thus, the concept of "academic discourses" refers to more that just the student's ability to produce standard English such as the correct phonology (sound system), lexicon (vocabulary), and syntax (sentence structure). In addition to these three language dimensions, less easily measured language components such as cultural knowledge about rhetorical structures (the ability to create texts whose logic and structure reflects academic and mainstream ways of organizing texts) are equally important. For example, one academic discourse strategy highly valued by educators is students' production of texts that reflect a unidimensional and linear line of argument.

Research by Gee[44] among others has shown that working-class African-American students often produce utterances in English that are difficult for their middle-class white teachers to understand. The communication difference often lies in the manner in which the students organize their texts and utilize contextual cues. For example, during sharing time Sarah Michaels[45] reports that middle-class white teachers often evaluated their African-American students' narratives as unwieldy, illogical, and confusing because the children produced oral text structures that did not follow a linear line of thought, assumed audience-shared background knowledge, and utilized culturally specific intonation cues to signal emphasis.

In the case of recently arrived immigrant students, the research suggests that older recently arrived immigrant students who received their elementary and secondary education in schools in their countries of origin often come to U.S. classrooms already possessing knowledge about academic rhetorical structures and communication practices valued in school contexts and necessary for success, particularly if they belong to a middle-class background. Although these students may be temporarily handicapped because of their limited English-language proficiency, once they acquire some threshold level in English, they eventually are able to transfer their native language academic discourse skills to English thus guaranteeing some degree of success in the classroom.[46]

Following this line of argument, it is likely that U.S. born and bred Mexican-American students often may not be similarly skilled as their Mexican-schooled counterparts because, unlike their Mexican-born peers, they usually have not had the opportunity to develop academic discourse skills in their primary language in a school context that supports their full linguistic development. The irony is that schools often require from these linguistic minority students precisely the academic discourse skills and knowledge bases they do not teach. It is what we call a "pedagogy of entrapment," in which even in contexts where teachers are well intentioned, they often fail to explicitly teach the academic discourse necessary for school success.

Even in bilingual classrooms designed to assist limited-English-proficient students' transition into English-only classrooms, teachers often make false assumptions concerning the level of linguistic minority students' English academic discourse abilities. One of these false assumptions is their failure to understand that academic discourse prerequisites are not inherently part of these students' working-class native-language competency. For example, most Mexican-American students in bilingual classrooms that have been studied come from a working-class reality and speak a variety of Spanish different from the Spanish academic discourse generally taught in bilingual programs. Thus, these students are often confronted with two major linguistic problems: their lack of proficiency in academic discourses of their second language, English, as well as their lack of academic proficiency in their native language, Spanish. Hence, to assume that these students will automatically transfer their presumed academic meta-linguistic awareness in the first language to the second represents a form of entrapment. One result is that many linguistic minority students in either English-only or bilingual settings are not being explicitly prepared to comprehend and produce more formal academic ways of speaking and writing in any language.

Academic Discourses and the Myth of "De-contextualized" Language

The very real pedagogical entrapment experienced by Mexican-American and other linguistic minority working-class-student populations contradicts much of the "common sense" presumption that in school settings teachers actually teach students more "academic ways" of communicating and yet the students fail to acquire these new linguistic strategies and structures. Unfortunately, while it is commonly accepted that academic discourses that rely on linguistic cues such as precise vocabulary and unilaterally structured syntactic and rhetorical structures are more communicatively efficient in an academic setting, the reality is that academic discourse conventions are seldom explicitly taught to working-class and linguistic minority students.[47] Furthermore, there is a tendency to glorify and romanticize a particular type of academic language—discourse that is referred to in the literature as "de-contextualized" language. Much of the current educational research identifies numerous linguistic features—all related to a text's overt levels of explicitness and implicitness in their operationalizaton of "decontextualized" language. Researchers' foci range from the use of lexical/prosodic cues, complexity of sentence structure, and the use of pronouns to texts' overall cohesiveness.[48]

Although this literature recognizes that, in reality, so-called decontextualized language is not truly *de*-contextualized, that is, devoid of all context, but rather, that it is contextualized using chiefly linguistic cues and strategies restricted to the text instead of relying on extralinguistic cues or cues located outside the sentence (such as use of body language, varying intonation, and assumptions of shared knowledge with interlocutors) to render a message explicit, it stops short of recognizing that these linguistic cues and strategies rely on values that become the contextual point of reference.

However, linguists such as James Gee are quick to point out that all language is contextualized and remind us of the culture-specific nature of using and valuing language that is linguistically contextualized. In fact, he specifically links children's ability to speak in "school-like" ways with their socialization in "school-like" home cultures:

> Certain cultures, as well as unschooled people in our culture, simply do not have, and do not use the conventions prevalent in our schools that in certain contrived situations (like "show and tell time") one pretends that people do not know or see what they obviously do know and see. . . . Such assumptions—that one should ignore what the hearer knows and explicitly say it anyway—are . . . the hallmark of many middle-class home-based practices with children (e.g., having the child repeat back an often read book or rehearse at the dinner table daily events that one already knows about). In other social groups . . . such explicitness may be seen as rude because it is distancing, blunt or condescending to the hearer's intelligence.[49]

Certain cultural and social groups place great value on producing texts that are overtly explicit and do not require interlocutor negotiation. That is, more middle-class and schooled ways of contextualizing text require distance among interlocutors so that key cues for making meaning are linguistic ones. One result of the popular use of the term "de-contextualized" is that it obfuscates the fact that the so-called de-contextualized language actually refers to language that utilizes the mainstream or dominant culture's preferred ways of contextualizing. We believe that the term "linguistically contextualized" constitutes a more accurate and objective descriptor of the type of language strategies we value in schools and does not perpetuate the erroneous almost mystical air that surrounds the term "de-contextualized language."

For example, the use of text organizing strategies such as the "topic-centered" organization of narratives that white middle-class children use (such as presenting a main point or theme and then elaborating about only that main point or theme) and the use of specific linguistic cues such as introductory sentences that inform the listener of the speaker's main point as well as his or her plans for organizing and presenting text are treated by the literature, not as culturally specific ways of contextualizing oral and written messages, but as text that is de-contextualized. Described as de-contextualized text, it is thus believed to be capable of transmitting meaning on its own irrespective of the context in which the communicative effort takes place.

Despite the *linguistic* reality that so-called de-contextualized language really is not free of all contextual information and cues, the *social* reality is that not all contextualizing conventions or strategies are perceived as equally valuable by the dominant culture. The use of linguistic cueing is perceived as more desirable and cognitively superior than extralinguistic structures and cueing systems (for example, body language and use of prosodic cues such as changing intonation). Here we begin to see how the dominant valuation system operates through distinction so as to asymmetrically distribute cultural goods.[50] In fact, even the so-called de-contextualized discourse relies on extralinguistic structures such as value systems to generate meaning. To a great extent, especially in classroom situations where students manage to communicate their intent, these preferences for form over content reflect social and cultural preferences rather than purely linguistic value.

These researchers, who in the name of science create (or sustain) a false dichotomy between "de-contextualized" and "contextualized" discourse, fail to realize not only that their coinage of these terms is false in that no discourse exists outside context but also that they play a key role in reproducing the dominant ideology that is often hidden by the very language they use to describe different linguistic varieties. The "de-contextualized" discourse implies linguistic superiority while making its context invisible. For instance, James Gee suggests that middle- and upper-class white college students answer questions on SAT tests without having to actually read the accompanying passages. In this study, Gee gave his students in an honors program (which is mostly populated by middle- and upper-middle-class white students) at the University of Southern California the following SAT questions.[51]

1. The main idea of the passage is that
    (A) a constricted view of [this novel] is natural and acceptable
    (B) a novel should not depict a vanished society
    (C) a good novel is an intellectual rather than an emotional experience
    (D) many readers have seen only the comedy [in this novel]
    (E) [this novel] should be read with sensitivity and an open mind
2. The author's attitude toward someone who enjoys [this novel] and then remarks "but of course it has no relevance today" (lines 21-22) can best be described as one of
    (A) amusement
    (B) astonishment
    (C) disapproval
    (D) resignation
    (E) ambivalence
3. The author [of this passage] implies that a work of art is properly judged on the basis of its
    (A) universality of human experience truthfully recorded
    (B) popularity and critical acclaim in its own age
    (C) openness to varied interpretations, including seemingly contradictory ones
    (D) avoidance of political and social issues of minor importance
    (E) continued popularity through different eras and with different societies.

Nearly 100 students who answered the above questions, answered them correctly 80 percent of the time without reading the accompanying passages. In fact, Gee argues that virtually no student has missed the answer to question 3 (which is A). However, when he gave the same questions to his "regular" undergraduate students (where there would be more diversity along class, race, and ethnicity), a great many more students answered them incorrectly.

What guides the students in the honors program to answer the questions correctly without reading the passages? Let's take question 3 to which the correct answer is A. According to Gee,

[A]vant-garde literary critics certainly do not believe that a work of art is properly judged on the basis of its universality of human experience truthfully recorded. In fact, they believe something much closer to answer C: A work of art is properly judged on the basis of its openness to varied interpretations, including seemingly contradictory ones. And my honors students do not, in fact, believe that a work of art is properly judged on the basis of its universality of human experience truthfully recorded, either. There are prone to believe something much closer to answer E: A work of art is properly judged on the basis of continued popularity through different eras and with different societies.

Why do my honors students answer A to question 3? They do so because they immediately recognize, in this question and the others, a certain set of values. They recognize a value like "truth and beauty transcend cultures," so they know that the answer to question 3 is A. They recognize a value like "truth and beauty transcend time," so they know that the answer to question 2 is C. And they recognize a value like "truth and beauty are open (and only open) to people who are appropriately sensitive and open minded" (that is, people who are not "ideological"), thus they know that the answer to question 1 is E.[52]

The SAT test experiment exemplifies that students who are socialized in a particular set of values that corresponds to those values held by the dominant institutions, such as schools and testing centers, among others, have no difficulty answering the test questions correctly even when they do not read the questions' accompanying passages or grapple with the test's so-called de-contextualized language. They do so because they are guided by a set of values required through their class and culture socialization rather than by any supernatural intelligence predisposition.

As Gee also correctly argues, these students even betray their own beliefs so as to adhere to what is believed to be a dominant consensus—a set of values shared by the dominant sector of the society. We would point out that the set of values that guide these students to the correct answers without their reading the questions represent a contextual point of reference for meaning making similar to the visible context-bound signposts used by working-class racial and ethnic students in meaning making. The difference is that in the so-called de-contextualized discourse, the point of reference is often made invisible in keeping with the inner workings of ideology. What is at work in the nomenclature of "de-contextualized discourse" is how students "respond appropriately to a specific hegemonic or displaced consensus centered on the values of dominant discourses, a consensus achieved among persons (in the dominant groups or not) whose paths through life have [for a time and place] fallen together with the members of these dominant Discourses."[53] Hence, the teaching and acquisition of dominant academic discourses requires much more than linguistic knowledge. It requires knowledge about "ways of being in the world, ways of acting, thinking, interacting, valuing, believing, speaking, and sometimes writing and reading, connected to particular identities and social roles."[54] If a teacher fails to acknowledge that certain groups of students who come from subordinated cultural and racial groups do not have access and membership to dominant discourses, this teacher not only is making the power of the dominant discourse invisible but he or she is reproducing the distinction (which often is invisible) inherent in the dominant discourses and that serve as a measure in the society as a whole. Thus, teaching and the acquisition of dominant discourses would inevitably involve democratizing social structures so that dominant academic discourses and the social, economic, and political structures they sustain become more accessible to subordinated students. Despite the ideological nature of these types of discourses, the operationalization of so-called de-contextualized language in the literature has tended to focus on solely linguistic features that render written and oral text overtly explicit by using precise vocabulary and syntax.

The Romanticization of Dominant Ways of Contextualizing

We believe that as educators committed to improving the academic achievement of linguistic minority students, and Mexican Americans, in particular, we need to investigate how and why the language and literacy practices exercised and the contextualizing strategies utilized by the schooled and socially powerful have come to be touted as inherently superior and desirable in comparison to those practiced by lower-status cultural groups. For example, it is important to understand that the practice of contextualizing language by relying chiefly on linguistic cues reflects Western European essayist or essay-text tradition.[55] Historically, oral language that resembles this type of written text organization has been heralded as more "logical" and desirable than less formal ways of structuring linguistic messages. Instead of recognizing the appropriateness (as well as the inappropriateness) of overtly explicit language in certain situations, the tendency has been to glorify this type of text organization, making ideological claims of the essay-text's superior value, whether in speech or writing, that become part of "'an armory of concepts, conventions and practices' that privilege one social formation as if it were natural, universal, or, at least, the end point of a normal developmental progression of cognitive skills."[56]

Thus, we strip so-called de-contextualized language of the almost magical properties attributed to it when we understand that, in reality, it refers to a speaker's and writer's ability to rely on linguistic cues to render language overtly explicit and precise. As mentioned earlier, researchers employ a variety of terms to describe oral and written language that rely primarily on linguistic cues for conveying meaning, because shared meaning between interlocutors cannot be assumed.

Thus, linguistic messages must be elaborated on in an overtly precise and explicit manner and in an almost metacognitive fashion so that the risk of misinterpretation is minimized.

It is useful to dissect the concept of linguistically contextualized language to understand that its high value in part reflects the dominant culture's preference for structuring and contextualizing language in ways that minimize the interlocutors' joint creation and negotiation of meaning. In academic settings, high value is placed on producing text that is linguistically contextualized, thus reducing the importance of and need for human interaction and negotiation of meaning.

Linguistically contextualized language thus becomes a kind of lingua franca in academic domains. Certainly, the ability to contextualize language by relying chiefly on textual features, especially in academic domains where individuals are expected to communicate with distant and unknown audiences, is a desired one. A set of agreed-upon contextualizing conventions becomes necessary for successful communication to take place. Rodino accurately describes the types of skills and thinking about language that students must possess in order to produce this academic lingua franca:

> Being removed from the face-to-face setting, and assuming no prior knowledge on the part of unsupportive interlocutors, [linguistically] contextualized language requires anticipating recipient's needs/expectation; filling in background information; assessing message effectiveness on-line; self-monitoring and self-repair; careful planning to achieve a coherent whole; using precise lexical reference; controlling the complex syntax necessary to make explicit all relationships between ideas, and to sustain lexicalized cohesion across the whole text.[57]

While it is important to recognize the value of this lingua franca in formal academic settings, we argue that instead of imbuing linguistically contextualized language with almost magical properties and denigrating students from cultural and social groups who generally do not rely on these types of contextualizing cues, it is important for educators of linguistic minority students to clearly comprehend the sociopolitical dimensions of language and literacy teaching so as to resist viewing dominant groups' uses of language as inherently superior and desirable, and to begin to identify ways for helping students in the critical appropriation of academic discourses.

The Devaluing of Nonacademic Ways of Contextualizing Language: Students' Response as Resistance

In addition to rendering "invisible" the contextualizing strategies of the mainstream, hence the term de-contextualized, there is a general tendency to make value judgments that adversely affect what is labeled contextualized language. Thus, language that is contextualized in para-linguistic ways and is generally spoken by nonmainstream populations is often viewed unfavorably. In other words, nonlinguistically contextualized language is often associated with the language variety spoken by groups that are generally relegated to the margins of the society. Thus, their linguistic production is not only devalued but is perceived as needing to undergo a "metamorphosis" of sorts into the standard discourse and text organization style, which is identified as de-contextualized.

The shift from a so-called context-bound to a seemingly de-contextualized discourse often involve psychological ramifications that can be far-reaching and yet are largely ignored by most teachers. For instance, the shift from a context-bound to a de-contextualized discourse can often be accompanied by the development or exacerbation of linguistic insecurity to the degree that students are encouraged to abandon and repress their so-called context-bound language, which is usually devalued by the standard middle-class-oriented curriculum. This form of linguistic coercion can produce linguistic resistance in students who begin to experience antagonism toward the academic discourses they are often cajoled into learning. By not understanding fully these psychological processes that are generally shaped by competing ideologies, teachers often fall into a binaristic position that does not bode well for a psychologically healthy pedagogy that is conducive to learning academic discourse. This lack of understanding of resistance often eclipses any possibility that teachers may detect linguistic resistance so they can mediate it and effectively teach the academic discourse while honoring the home discourses of their students.

We are reminded of a story told by Dell Hymes (personal communication 1989), a respected anthropologist and educator, that illustrates our point. During the early sixties, while he was a professor at the Harvard Graduate School of Education, Hymes was recruited to help solve educational problems experienced by students in a Boston public elementary school that was located next to what was then the poorest and most dangerous housing project in Boston, populated mostly by African-Americans. The school was almost 100 percent African-American, while over 95 percent of the teaching staff and administration were middle-class white.

Hymes put into place mechanisms that encouraged and facilitated African-American parents' involvement in the schools. These mechanisms also enabled teachers to familiarize themselves with the cultural backgrounds of the students they were teaching. Many African-American mothers became teacher's aides and helped bridge the gap between the school and the community. During one of the teacher-parent meetings, a well-meaning white, middle-class teacher commented on her students' inability to learn standard English: "I have tried everything under the sun. I have gone downtown to buy colorful books, I have bought crayons, I use overheads, and these students still don't seem to be able to learn the standard." She was interrupted by an African-American mother who was serving as an aide in her classroom: "Ma'am, I'm sorry, but I have to disagree with you. When I take these students outside for recess, and when they play school, when they role play the teacher, they speak exactly like you do."[58]

Here you have a case in which students as young as seven or eight years old have, albeit unconsciously, began to resist performing in the academic discourse in the classroom, although they are fully able to do so when the white, middle-class teacher is absent. This example illustrates how students whose language and culture are devalued by schools generally develop resistance mechanisms to protect their

already fractured culture from the symbolic and real violence perpetrated against their cultural reality by the white middle-class school
culture.

The blind imposition of the so-called de-contextualized academic
discourse not only reproduces the false assumption that academic discourses are not context bound, it also functions as a measure against
which students' contextualization of their language is devalued, producing potentially serious psychological scars, even in students who
come to fully master academic discourses and become highly successful professionals. For example, according to José Cárdenas (personal
communication, 1980), former director of the Intercultural Development Research Association in San Antonio, Texas, his school experience was not only linguistically traumatic, but also left him with
identifiable psychological scars: "I still remember it, not as an uncomfortable, unpleasant, or challenging situation, but, rather, as a traumatic, disconcerting, terrorizing experience."By not understanding
the psychological ramifications, teachers more often than not blame
the students for their failure, rather than examining the erroneous
assumptions that inform their pedagogy including that which is pred-
icated on the false dichotomy between context-bound versus de-contextualized discourse. It is not true that minority students cannot
learn standard academic discourses, as demonstrated by the Hymes
example and by José Cárdenas. The problem lies with the "traumatic,
disconcerting, terrorizing experience" that generally leads minority
students to find refuge in linguistic resistance to the imposition and
promotion of what has been characterized by the dominant school
culture as de-contextualized language.

Conclusion

As we have attempted to demonstrate, before we can announce the
existence of multicultural programs fully based on a truly cultural
democracy (this obviously would involve languages as factors of culture), we need to dennounce the false assumptions and naïveté that
often lead to a form of charitable paternalism. However, to denounce
invariably involves courage, which, unfortunately, is in short supply.

As coauthor Donaldo Macedo recounts, during a conference in which he attempted to unmask the dominant ideology mechanisms involved in the present assault on bilingual education, a woman approached him and said: "Thank you very much for your courage to say things that many of us are too afraid to say." Since he was taken by surprise, he did not know how to respond but managed to make a point with the following question: Isn't it ironic that in a democracy to speak the truth, at least one's truth, one must have courage to do so? She squeezed his hand and politely said good-bye. After she left, Macedo began to think that what he should have told her is that to advocate for the democratic rights of bilingual students and to denounce the inequities that shape their (mis)education, "it is not necessary to be courageous; it is enough to be honest."[59] And to be honest would require that we denounce those reactionary educators who believe that bilingual education "is highly contentious and politicized . . . and there is a lack of clear consensus about the advantages and disadvantages of academic instruction in the primary language in contrast to early and intensive exposure to English."[60] To be honest would also require that we denounce the research industry that makes a living by pointing out the "lack of clear consensus" in the bilingual debate without providing alternative pedagogies that would effectively address the specificities of needs among linguistic minority students while the same research industry remains complicit with the very oppressive structures responsible for the poverty and human misery that characterize the lives of a large segment of linguistic minority students who go to inner-city public schools. Let's take the Head Start research. Many white Head Start researchers are rewarded by the dominant ideology for their complicity with the doctrinal system. They are again rewarded through large grant awards to study the early exposure to literacy as a compensation for the poverty and savage inequalities with which many of these white researchers remain in total complicity. Often, these studies end up stating the obvious, pointing to the proverbial "lack of clear consensus," which, in turn, calls for more research. While the call for more research ultimately benefits the researchers themselves, it invariably takes away precious resources that could be spent to diminish the adverse consequences of the savage inequalities that inform the lives of most minority children. To be honest would require that reactionary educators acknowledge the existence of the intimate interrelationship between society's discriminatory practices and the "savage inequalities" that shape the (mis)education of linguistic minority students. This would, invariably, point to the political nature of education that reactionary educators call "politicizing" education.

"Politicizing" education becomes a negative "shock word" to muffle rigorous academic debate concerning both the grievances and the educational needs of linguistic minority students. Only through a thorough deconstruction of the ideology that prevents linguistic minority students' sociocultural reality from becoming an area of serious inquiry can, for example, educators who want to falsely take politics out of education learn that it is erroneous to think that "[s]peaking a non standard variety of English can impede the easy acquisition of English literacy by introducing greater deviations in the representation of sounds, making it hard to develop sound symbol links."[61] This position makes the assumption that standard dialects are monolithic and show no phonological variations, which, in turn, restricts the "deviations in the representation of sounds, making it [easier] to develop sound-symbol links." Such posture is sustained only by a folk theory believed only by nonlinguists. Anyone who has been exposed to the Boston dialect notices that its speakers almost always drop the phoneme /r/ in the final position as in car, yet middle-class speakers of such dialect have little difficulty linking the dropped phoneme /r/ and its respective graphemic representation. This form of folk theory is possible due to the present excess in positivism whereby numbers are elevated to an almost mythical status which, in turn, dismisses other fundamental factors that have important pedagogical implications that remain largely ignored. For example, as Celia T. Leyva recounts:

[G]rowing up, I was often reprimanded for speaking Spanish in class and even in the lunch room, and also discriminated against because I spoke English with a Cuban accent. I was ridiculed not only by classmates, but also by my teachers who insisted that I had to speak English like Americans do. Because of the humiliation I went through growing up, I felt the need to prevent my own children from similar situations, and robbed them of the opportunity to learn my native language and, at the same time denied them their own culture. I hated English and I hated learning it."[62]

Perhaps more so than the mere ability to link sound and symbol in English, factors such as linguistic and cultural resistance play a great role in the acquisition of the dominant standard English. bell hooks painfully acknowledges that the dominant standard English, far from being seen as a neutral tool of communication, for most African-Americans, is viewed as the "oppressor's language [which] has the potential to disempower those of us who are just learning to speak, who are just learning to claim language as a place where we make ourselves subject."[63]

In learning the "oppressor's language," we are often forced to experience subordination in speaking it. Upon reflection, bell hooks states that "it is not the English language that hurt me, but what the oppressors do with it, how they shape it to become a territory that limits and defines , how they make it a weapon that can shame, humiliate, colonize."[64] We would argue that the shaming, humiliation, and colonization nonspeakers of the dominant standard English feel in their relationship with English have a great deal more to do with the lack of reading success in the standard English than the mechanical struggles these students face in making sense of sound-symbol link due to unavoidable phonological variations found in all dialects, including the dominant standard English. The nature of the nonstandard variety does not determine the subordinate students' inability to learn the ABCs, which, in turn, warrants that they be taught "how to learn." These students have little difficulty learning what the chief of psychiatry at San Diego's Children's Hospital rightly describes as the "more relevant skills of the DBSs (drive-by-shootings)"[65] and other survival skills, which are vividly and painfully mastered by any student whose reality is characterized by violence, human misery, and despair.

To be honest would require that we reconnect with history so as to learn from the thousands of Chicano high school students who, in 1968, walked out of their respective high schools as a protest against their miseducation. They walked out to demand quality education, cultural dignity, and an end to cultural violence. The passion, courage, and determination those Chicano students demonstrated will serve us well again as we attempt to refigure how to best educate linguistic minority students. Their courage, passion, and determination energized educators, political leaders, and community activists to coalesce so to address the urgent needs that Chicanos as well as other linguistic minority students were facing then. The needs of linguistic minority students are in a sense greater today given the added vicious assault on bilingual education. For this reason, teachers, parents, researchers, and community members need to again coalesce with the same determination to not only provide quality education to linguistic minority students but also to work aggressively to dismantle the social and cultural fabric that informs, shapes, and reproduces the despair of poverty, fatalism, and hopelessness. To be honest would require that white liberals as well as conservative educators understand the underlying ideology in their assumption that what Latinos need is basic research. We counter this argument by saying that what Latinos need is social justice and cultural and economic equity.

By incorporating linguistic minority students' cultural and linguistic processes into forms of textual, social, and political analysis, educators will not only develop means to counter the dominant attempt to impose English as the only educational practice, but they will also equip themselves with the necessary tools to embrace a pedagogy of hope based on cultural production where specific groups of people produce, mediate, and confirm the mutual ideological elements that emerge from and affirm their cultural experiences. These include, obviously, the languages though which these experiences are reflected and refracted. Only through experiences that are rooted in the interests of individual and collective self-determination can we create democratic education. Cultural production, not reproduction by imposing English, is the only means through which we can achieve a true cultural democracy. In this sense, bilingual education offers us not only with a great opportunity to democratize our schools but "is itself a utopian pedagogy."[66] By the very fact that it is a utopian pedagogy, according to Paulo Freire,

> it is full of hope, for to be utopian is not to be merely idealistic or impractical but rather to engage in denunciation and annunciation. Our pedagogy cannot do without a vision of man [and woman] of the world. It formulates a scientific humanist conception that finds its expression in a dialogical praxis in which the teachers and learners together, in the act of analyzing a dehumanizing reality, denounce it while announcing its transformation in the name of the liberation of man [and woman]."[67]

Notes

1. Albert Memmi, *The Colonizer and the Colonized* (Boston: Beacon Press, 1967), p. 107.
2. Alan Lupo, "Accentuating the Negative," *Boston Globe*, March 4, 1992, p. 19.
3. "Humanities 101, Westfield style," *Boston Globe*, March 3, 1992, p. 16.
4. Mihailo Markovic, Liubomir Tadic and Danko Grlik, *Liberalismo y Socialismo: Teoria y Praxis* (Mexico: Editorial Grijalbo, 1977), p. 19.
5. Ibid., p. 17.
6. Geralso Navas Davilla, *La Dialectica del Desarrollo Nacional: El caso de Puerto Rico* (San Juan: Editorial Universitaria, 1978), p. 27.
7. Renato Constantino, *Neocolonial Identity and Counter-Consciousness* (London: Merlin Press, 1978), p. 66.
8. Ibid., p. 67.
9. Maria M. Lopez Lagunne, *Bilingualismo en Puerto Rico: Actitudes Sociolinguisticas del Maestro* (San Juan: M.I.S.C.E.S., Corp., 1989), p. 17.
10. H. Eysenck, *The IQ argument: Race, Intelligence, and Education* (New York: Library Press, 1971).
11. Zeynep F. Beykont, "Academic Progress of a Nondominant Group: A Longitudinal Study of Puerto Ricans in New York City's Late Exit Bilingual Programs," doctoral dissertation, Harvard University, 1994. Virginia P. Collier, "A Synthesis of Studies Examining Long-term Language Minority Student Data on Academic Achievement." *Bilingual Research Journal*, 16, no. 182, (1992), pp. 187-212. James Cummins, "The Role of Primary Language Development in Promoting Educational Success for Language Minority Students," in California State Department of Education (ed.), *Schooling and Language Minority Students: A Theoretical Framework.* Evaluation, Dissemination and Assessment Center, California State University, Los Angeles, 1982. Kenji Hakuta, *Mirror of Language: The Debate on Bilingualism* (New York: Basic Books, 1986).

12. Pepi Leistyna, *Presence of Mind: Education and Politics of Deception* (Boulder, CO: Westview Press, 1998).

13. Carry Nelson, *Manifesto of a Tenured Radical* (New York: New York University Press, 1997), p. 19.

14. Ibid.

15. Henry A. Giroux, *Theory and Resistance: A Pedagogy for the Opposition* (South Hadley, MA: J. F. Bergin, 1983), p. 87.

16. Michael Schudson, *Discovering the News: A Social History of American Newspapers* (New York: Basic Books, 1978), p. 6.

17. Ibid.

18. "Bilingual Grads Outperform Others in 2 Districts," *San Diego Union Tribune*, July 8, 1998, p. 143.

19. For a comprehensive and critical discussion of scientific objectivity, see Donna Haraway, "Situated Knowledges: The Science Question in Feminism and the Privilege of Partial Perspectives," *Feminist Studies* 14 (1988): pp. 575-599.

20. Linda Brodkey, *Writing Permitted in Designated Areas Only* (St. Paul: Minnesota University Press, 1966), p. 10.

21. Ibid., p. 8.

22. Ibid.

23. Roger Fowler et al., *Language and Control* (London: Routledge & Keagan Paul, 1979), p. 192.

24. Greg Myers, "Reality, Consensus, and Reform in the Rhetoric of Composition Teaching," *College English* 48, no. 2 (February 1986).

25. Jonathan Kozol, *Amazing Grace: The Lines and the Conscience of a Nation* (New York: Harper Perennial, 1996), p. 4.

26. Ibid., p. 39.

27. Richard J. Hernstein and Charles Murray, *The Bell Curve: Intelligence and Class Structure in American Life* (New York: The Free Press, 1994).

28. Henry A. Giroux, *Theory and Resistence*, p. 87.

29. Paulo Freire, *Pedagogy of Freedom: Ethics, Democracy, and Civic Courage* (Boulder, CO: Rowman & Littlefield Publishers, 1998).

30. Ibid.

31. Gloria Anzaldúa. *Borderlands: The New Mestiza* (San Francisco: Spinsters/Aunt Lute, 1987), p. 203.

32. Ibid.

33. Ladislaus Semali and Joe L. Kincheloe (eds.) *What is Indigenous Knowledge and Why Should We Study It?*

34. Joseph H. Suina, "And Then I Went to School," in Rodney R. Cocking and Jose P. Mestre (eds.), *Linguistic and Cultural Influences on Learning Mathematics* (Hillsdale, NJ: Lawrence Erlbaum Associates Publishers, 1998), p. 297.

35. Ngugi Wa Thiong'o. *Decolonizing the Mind: The Politics of Language in African Literature* (Portsmouth: NH: Heinemann Press, 1986), p. 11.

36. Henry A. Giroux and Peter McLaren, "Teacher Education and the Politics of

Engagement: The Case for Democratic Schooling," *Harvard Educational Review* 56, no. 3 (August 1986), p. 213-238.

37. Mikhail Bakhtin, *The Dialogic Imagination*, trans. Caryl Emerson and Michael Holquist (Austin: University of Texas Press, 1981), p. 294.

38. Václav Havel, *Living in Truth* (London: Faber and Faber, 1989), p. 42.

39. Jean-Paul Sartre, introduction to *The Colonizer and the Colonized*, by Albert Memmi Boston: Beacon Press, 1967), pp. xxiv-xxv.

40. Ibid., p. xxvi.

41. Stanley Arronowitz, "Between Nationality and Class," *Harvard Educational Review* vol. 67, no 2 (1997) p. 202.

42. Gloria Anzaldua "How to Tame a Wild Tongue," *Borderlands: The New Mestiza* (San Francisco: Spinsters/Aunt Lute, 1987), p. 207.

43. James Paul Gee, "What is Literacy?" in C. Mitchell and K. Weiler (eds.), *Rewriting Literacy: Culture and the Discourse of the Other* (South Hadley, MA: Bergin & Garvey Publishers, 1991) p. 3.

44. James Paul Gee, *Sociolinguistics and Literacies: Ideologies in Discourses* (London, Falner Press, 1990), p. 3.

45. Sarah Michaels, "Nonnative Presentations: An Oral Preparation for Literacy and First Graders" in J. Cook Gumperz (ed.) *The Social Construction of Literacy* (New York: Cambridge University Press, 1986), pp. 94-116.

46. Cummins, James. "The Role of Primary Language Development in Promoting Educational Success for Language Minority Students."

47. Delpit, L., *Other People's Children: Cultural Conflict in the Classroom* (New York: The New Press, 1995).

48. Ibid.

49. James Paul Gee. *Sociolinguistics and Literacies*, p. 60.

50. Pienne Bourdieu. *Language and Symbolic Power* (Cambridge, MA: Harvard University Press, 1991).

51. James Paul Gee. "Reading" in *Journal of Urban and Cultural Studies*, 2 no. 2, (1992), pp. 65-77.

52. Ibid., pp. 66-77.

53. Ibid., p. 74.

54. Ibid., p. 73.

55. James Paul Gee. *Sociolinguistics and Literacies*, p 60.

56. Ibid.

57. A. M. Rodina, "y . . . No Puedo Decir mas na," in *"The Maintenance of Native Language Skills by Working Class Puerto Ricans in Mainland Schools*, qualifying paper, Harvard Graduate School of Education.

58. E. S. Anderson, *Speaking with Style: The Sociolinguistic Skills of Children* (New York: Routledge Press, 1987).

59. Amilcar Cabral, *Return to the Source* (New York and London: Monthly Review Press, 1974), p. 16.

60. Catherine E. Snow, M. Susan Burns, and Peg Griffin (eds). *Committee on the*

Prevention of Reading Difficulties in young Children (Washington, DC: 1998), p. 29.

61. Ibid., pp. 27-28.
62. Celia T. Leyva, "Language Philosophy Research Paper" presented to a graduate class in sociolinguistics, University of Massachusetts Boston, fall 1998.
63. bell hooks, *Teaching to Transgress* (New York: Routledge, 1996), p. 168.
64. Ibid., p. 168.
65. Saul Levine, "On Guns and Health Care: The U.S. Caves In to Force," *San Diego Union Tribune*, August 12, 1993, p.11.
66. Paulo Freire, *The Politics of Education: Culture, Power and Liberation* (New York: Bergin and Garvey Publishers, 1985), p. 57.
67. Ibid.

CHAPTER 3

RACISM AS A CULTURAL FACTOR
A Dialogue with Paulo Freire

> *I will say, then, that I am not, nor ever have been in favor of bringing about in any way the social and political equality of white and black races. . . . I as much as any other man am in favor of having the superior position assigned to the white race.*
> —Abraham Lincoln

So far, we have proposed that in order to understand the systematic devaluation of "otherness" along the lines of race, culture, and ethnicity, we need to critically examine the colonial legacy that continually undermines our democratic aspirations. However, to do so would require that we reconnect with our past so as to critically understand that beneath the aura of democracy lies a colonial historical will that has bequeathed us the rampant social inequality that exists today. Once we become cognizant of the colonial ideology that still informs our so-called democratic society, we can begin to create structures that will lead to a total decolonization so as to achieve a truly cultural democracy.

The paradox facing many multicultural educators, with the exception of some critical multiculturalists, is that they naively, but not innocently, allowed themselves to fall prey to a false historical discontinuity between our colonial past and a "deferred" democracy paralyzed by racism. This form of paralysis is not, however, dissimilar from the colonial framework whereby "all the efforts of the colonialist are directed toward maintaining this social inability, and racism is the surest weapon for this aim."[1] It is precisely because of the colonial ideology that conservative educators and political pundits attempt to keep the colonial legacy that informs their attack on multiculturalism hidden and outside the public debate. By so doing, on the one hand, they attempt to maintain the pillars of the colonial system that can only be sustained on an unstable foundation of lies, and on the other hand, they seek to prevent the revealing of the racist fabric of our democracy, for such a revelation would open the possibility of imagining a society that is less discriminatory and more just, less dehumanizing and more humane. That is why many conservative educators, including some facile liberals, decry the push for multiculturalism, as it calls into question Western cultural hegemony and the barbarism Western cultures committed against other cultural groups in the name of "civilizing" the "barbaric" other. Thus, cultural commissars such as Dinesh D'Souza writes a book proclaiming the end of racism while some liberal apologists contend that we have made great strides since the civil rights movement and racism is not as bad as it used to be. This attitude represents a form of false benevolence that was characteristic of the colonizer's paternalistic mental attitude. According to Albert Memmi,

> A paternalistic is one who wants to stretch racism and inequality farther—once admitted. It is, if you like, a charitable racism—which is not thereby less skillful nor less profitable. For the most generous paternalism results as soon as the colonized demands his union rights, for example. If he increases his wages, if his wife looks after the colonized, these are gifts and never duties, he would have to admit that the colonized have rights. But it is clear from everything above that he has no duties and the colonized have no rights.[2]

It is not surprising that while we are witnessing increased proclamation concerning the end of racism, we are likewise observing a corresponding increase of attacks on affirmative action and other legislative mechanisms designed to guarantee that the oppressed in our society have equal access to jobs and schools from which they were legally excluded. In many ways, a large segment of our society view affirmative actions as "gifts and never duties." Even in liberal institutions where many liberals would defend affirmative action as a process to engender diversity, affirmative action rarely applies to high-level management. Take for example universities that pride them-selves on their commitment to diversity where diversity is often skewed toward the lower rung of institutional life. Thus, it is common to find universities with a proclaimed commitment to diversity enrolling students who come from diverse backgrounds while their faculty remain almost exclusively white. As we move upward in the institutional hierarchy of these universities, the hegemony of white power becomes undeniable. When universities appoint, let's say, non-white deans, often as tokens, great care is taken to be sure that too many of them are not given these positions of power. Hence, it is common to hear comments such as "we already have an African-American dean" or "we already have a Latino professor in the depart-ment." This very discourse betrays the claim for cultural and racial diversity while it unveils the racist ideology that is often sugarcoated by a banal claim for a tokenistic diversity. While the African-American deans or two or three Latino professors may be considered too many by those who consider themselves pro-diversity, these same individu-als remain indifferent if, let's say, the administrations is composed mainly of white administrators, and often mostly white men.

As we move away from the window-dressing diversity and analyze the very discourse that sustains the tokenistic diversity, we begin to understand the ambivalence that is characteristic of present debate on cultural diversity. For example, when African-Americans and other minority administrators compete and demonstrate higher compe-tence for the job, it is not uncommon to hear the following. "If she is hired as a chancellor, she will unleash all kinds of political agendas."

It is as if a white male chancellor has, by virtue of his race and sex-ual makeup, no political agenda. Thus, white men and women are, politically speaking, always agendaless while people of color are, by their very racial or ethnic location, promoters of political agendas. The insidiousness of such racist ideology often betrays even those white liberals who love to wear their nonracist badge on their sleeves always. Let us analyze the discourse of a liberal white man while assessing the risks of hiring a Latina provost. While acknowledging that the Latina had extraordinarily impressed everyone in the search committee, and had demonstrated superior knowledge of higher education, particularly public higher education, and she embodied the values of the institution, he, however, cautioned that hiring the Latina as provost for the university would constitute a real risk. According to him, "if she failed, it would be a total failure." As if the failures of a white men or white women in such positions are never total. In essence, he was right to the extent that we often soften the failures of white administrators while remaining always unforgiving and critical of minority failures.

What these discourse analyses point to is that while we can conceive of diversity that never threatens our privilege in that we are always in a position to manage diversity (the case of white professors claiming to love diversity of students in their classes) we are still unable to imagine ourselves being managed by diversity. In other words, diversity is good so long it remains charitable and never threatens the privileged positions of white men and women. These examples also illustrate that "racism sums up and symbolizes the fundamental relation which unites colonialist and colonized."[3] In our democratic society, it "sums up and symbolizes the fundamental relation" between the whites and nonwhites.

Our lack of understanding regarding the colonial legacy that informs and shapes the cruel and often violent racist reality which characterizes our democratic society is mainly due to a colonial ideology that, in order to preserve and reproduce itself, relies on three major mechanisms: "one, the gulf between the culture of the colonialist and the colonized; two, the exploitation of these differences for the benefit of the colonialist; three, the use of those supposed differences as standards of absolute fact."[4] These ideological components are not dissimilar from the mechanisms used in our society to produce and reproduce the white supremacy ideology. In addition, the reproduction of both a colonialist and white supremacist ideology is often achieved through the dehistoricization of the colonized and oppressed contexts. Thus, a false rupture in historical continuity that denies the oppressed both his or her rights as a historical subject and ways to access knowledge about how he or she became a historical object represent an ideological tool, par excellence, often used by the dominant ideology to suppress, repress, devalue, disconfirm, and dehumanize the colonized and the oppressed. It is, therefore, not a surprise that in both the colonial context and in our contemporary racist democracy we are not given much opportunity to reconnect with our historical past so as to understand the colonial legacy that promotes, shapes, and sustains the racist fabric of our society. Although Renato Constantino was writing about the colonial legacy in the Philippines, his thoughtful words are not only apropos but also illuminating regarding the present historical juncture in our society:

> We see our present with as little understanding as we view our past because aspects of the past which could illumine the present have been concealed from us. This concealment has been effected by a systemic process of mis-education characterized by a thoroughgoing inculcation of colonial values and attitudes—a process which could not have been so effective had we not been denied access to the truth and to be part of our written history. As a consequence, we have become a people without a sense of history. We accept the present as given, bereft of historicity. Because we have so little comprehension of our past, we have no appreciation of its meaningful interrelation with the present.[5]

This concealment of history so as to deny us a critical comprehension of our past is part and parcel of the dominant ideological mechanisms designed to enable cultural commissars who often work to legitimize the oppressive nature of the dominant ideology. They not only attempt to make the dominant ideology commonsense in the Gramscian perspective but also force us to accept the present as given and immobile. Thus, it is not at all surprising that we cannot detect the historical continuity between the white supremacist ideology contained in Galton's *Hereditary Genius,* written in 1869, and the *Harvard Educational Review*'s resurrection of the same racist ideology with the publication of Arthur Jensen's article " How Much Can We Boost IQ and Scholastic Achievement?" It is the same historical amnesia that forces us to detour around the racist dominant ideology with little appreciation of the significance and meaningfulness of the media hype surrounding the publication of *The Bell Curve,* which included coverage from *Newsweek* to *Time* magazine to "Nightline and showing up on the shelves of K-Marts all over the country."[6] In the dialogue that follows we attempt to understand how ideological manipulation of history hides the racist fabric of our society behind the facade of democracy that, in turn, enable us to maintain some form of dignity in our eternal dance with bigotry.

Macedo: If it were not for the amnesia prevalent within U.S. society, it would be very easy to understand that the present cruel and frontal attack on affirmative action, immigrants, and unwed mothers, etc., is a mere continuation of a historical context where blacks were "scientifically" relegated to a subhuman existence, which, in turn, justified the irrationality of their alienating reality as slaves. After the abolition of slavery and with the eradication of laws that protected the existence of slavery, the dominant white ideology resorted to "science" as a means not only to demonize but also to dehumanize blacks in the United States. These race-based ideological mechanisms were very much prominent during the Reconstruction as succinctly described by a black historian of the era, W. E. B. DuBois:

> The South proved by appropriate propaganda the Negro government was the worst ever seen and that it threatened civilization. They suited their propaganda to their audience. They had tried the accusation of laziness but that was refuted by a restoration of agriculture to the pre-war level and beyond it. They tried the accusation of ignorance, but this was answered by the Negro schools.
>
> It happened that the accusation of incompetence impressed the North. . . . Because the North had never been thoroughly converted to the idea of Negro equality. . . .
>
> Did the nation want blacks with power sitting in the Senate and the House of Representatives, accumulating wealth and entering the learned professions? Would this not eventually and inevitably lead to social equality? Was it possible to contemplate such eventualities?

Under such circumstances, it was much easier to believe the accusations of the South and to listen to the proof which biology and social science hastened to adduce the inferiority of the Negro. The North seized upon the new Darwinism, "the survival of the fittest," to prove that what they had attempted in the South was an impossibility; and they did this in the face of the facts before them, the examples of Negro efficiency, of Negro brains, of phenomenal possibilities of advancement.[7]

Sadly, after over one century, the United States continues to be embroiled in the debate centered on the false notion of the genetic inferiority of blacks. The publication of the book *The Bell Curve,* by Charles Murray and Richard J. Hernstein, once more presents "evidence" in support of genetic inferiority. This book has not only activated what had appeared to be a dormancy of racism in the United States after the enactment of the civil rights laws, but it also has resurrected an old form of intellectual lynching that, unfortunately, has been embraced by ever more powerful representatives of the far right and, with some exception, by liberals through a form of silence. Paulo, can you comment on the reemergence of the legitimization of racism through pseudoscientific methods?

Freire: When I am confronted with the problem of racial discrimination, independently of the insidious explanations that a racist pretends to give in order to maintain his or her attitude that negates the existence and equal rights of the other, my first reaction is one of anger mixed with pity. By pity I am not referring to the victims of discrimination. I pity those who discriminate. I pity their lack of human sensibility. I pity their exaggerated arrogance with respect to the world and their lack of humility.

These expressions of both anger and pity are obviously understood by those who discriminate, particularly those who use pseudoscience to legitimatize their racism, as empty platitudes, empty and incompetent discourses. But, for me, the use of science to prove the inferiority of blacks is also an incompetent discourse. Between these two incompetent discourses, I prefer the humanism and humility that exist in my position.

I remember very well when I was at Harvard and a professor there published an infamous and highly controversial article in the *Harvard Education Review*. In this article, the author, Arthur Jensen, argued that he would be more than happy to say that there is no racial inferiority between races, but science would not permit him to do so, since, according to his calculations, blacks are inferior, even though they excel in their ability as runners. When I think about the reaction I had when I read his argument, I feel the same way today when the authors of *The Bell Curve* strive to resurrect the mechanism of dehumanization parading, once again, under the veil of science.

Another thing that I want to point out is that when I oppose these pseudo-scientists and their scientism for their cruel and racist approach to scholarship, I remain unafraid of being criticized for not having a scientific basis on which to make such a claim. I would like to say here, to proclaim, if you will, that there is no other basis on which to judge one another, than upon the basis of membership in the human race. I am not interested in going to a laboratory in an effort to attempt to prove that blacks are inferior to whites or vice versa. I find this pseudoscientific endeavor absurd. It is absurd to claim the inferiority of human beings because of their historical accident of birth along the lines of race, gender, and ethnicity. If there is one thing that distinguishes humans from animals, as Francois Jacoby notes, it is our innate ability to learn. This is, in my view, scientific affirmation. It is not a mere dream to say that we are beings who are programmed to know and to learn. Jensen, Murray, Hernstein, and others would have to demonstrate that blacks are programmed to know and learn less than whites. I would argue otherwise. Even if their claim were to be scientifically true, there would have to be no exceptions to the rule. In other words, we could not have a W. E. B. DuBois, a Martin Luther King, a Toni Morrison, a Nelson Mandela among a constellation of great black leaders and intellectuals in the world. If the claim of inferiority were to be true, all blacks in the world would have to be inferior in all domains and respects, in both time and space. They would have to be inferior ethically, aesthetically, physically, and so forth. In fact, this never is the case. If, in fact, blacks were genetically inferior, Amilcar Cabral, the leader of the movement for the independence of Guinea-Bissau and Cape Verde would not have created so many problems for the Portuguese government and, indirectly, its supporter, the United States. Amilcar Cabral and his black army defeated completely the Portuguese white army. When I say Amilcar Cabral, I also have in mind other African leaders and their people who also defeated the European colonizers. It was the African intelligence and its ethical conscience that enabled the indigenous population to reacquire not only its land but also its human dignity by removing the yoke of a vicious colonialism. It is this intelligence that triumphed over the human exploitation, the dehumanization, the cowardice, and deceitful attitudes of the European colonizers. The Africans won the war and the Europeans had to flee.

Macedo: Let me interrupt you for a moment. I think it is important not only to point out the Africans' intelligence in devising battle field strategies that led to the defeat of European colonialism, but is also crucial that the ethical and moral issues involved in the struggle for independence be analyzed. In other words, how can the Europeans, who, according to these pseudoscientists, are holders of superior intelligence, this civilization, justify the dehumanizing effects of colonialism and the barbaric and cruel atrocities committed by them in their pursuit of ways to satiate their greed. As supposedly superior and more civilized beings, how can Europeans justify their quasi-genocide inherent in the process of colonialization designed to secure and help them consolidate European cultural hegemony. If the white race is intellectually superior and, in turn, supposedly represents the bastion of civilization, how can these pseudoscientists justify the worldwide human exploitation engineered by whites, the mass killings of elderly, women, and children by our Western developed smart bombs, the mass killing and raping of women, including children as young as five years old in Bosnia, as Western civilization watches from the sidelines? The supposed white European superiority is directly compromised in the following historical observation:

> If you were a colonist, you knew that your technology was superior to the Indians: You knew that you were civilized, and they were savages. . . . But your superior technology proved insuffi-

cient to extract anything. The Indians, keeping to themselves, laughed at your superior methods and lived from the land more abundantly and with less labor than you did. . . . And when your own people started deserting in order to live with them, it was too much . . . so you killed the Indians, tortured them, burned their villages, burned their corn fields. It proved your superiority, in spite of your failures. And you gave similar treatment to any of your own people who succumbed to their savage ways of life. But you still did not grow much corn.[8]

How can Charles Murray and his cultural legionnaires justify the superiority of the white race, when technology and military intelligence fashioned by whites leads American GIs to commit horrendous crimes against humanity as described by Vietnam veterans themselves:

The girls were unconscious at that point [after repeated rapes]. When they finished raping them, three of the GIs took hand flares and shoved them in the girls' vaginas. . . . No one needed to hold them down any longer. The girls were bleeding from their mouths, noses, faces and vaginas. Then they struck the exterior portion of the flares and they exploded inside the girls. Their stomachs started bloating up and they exploded. The stomachs exploded and their intestines were just hanging out of their bodies.[9]

If Murray, Hernstein, and Jensen, among others, were to be true to the claim of the objectivity of their science, they would factor in why the higher white IQ predisposed the white civilization to commit grotesque, barbaric, and horrendous crimes against humanity as has been the case throughout history. It is precisely because of these pseudoscientists' selective selection of historical facts in their determination of IQ that we need to keep dangerous historical memories alive as reminders of the consequences of all forms of dehumanization, particularly the type of dehumanization sanctioned by science. It is for this reason that for each Museum of Fine Arts we build in a given city, we should also build a museum of slavery with graphic accounts of the dehumanization of African-Americans, when entire families were split and sold on the block to the highest bidder and where pictures of lynching would remind us of our racist fabric. For each museum of science built in a given city, we should also build a museum of the quasi-genocide of American Indians, their enslavement, the raping and killing of their women, and the appropriation of their land. Although we have built a Holocaust Museum in Washington, D.C., fifty years after the Nazis' horrendous crimes against Jews, Gypsies, and Communists, we also need to build a Vietnam War Museum along with the Vietnam Memorial, where graphic accounts of rape and killing of Vietnamese women, children, and innocent elderly by Western-heritage-trained GIs would be described, thus keeping the dangerous memories of My Lai alive.

Although the existence of these museums would represent historical truths, I doubt it very much that our society is willing to confront its demons, as exemplified in the watering down and rewriting of history in the case of the exhibition of the *Enola Gay* at the Smithsonian. After ferocious protests by veteran's groups, the exhibition not only brooked no historical analysis, it also suppressed historical truths, rendering the exhibition to a mere presentation of artifacts without any connection with historical analysis.

For me, more important than proving white IQ superiority is the design of scientific studies that engage students in the archaeology of a white generic map that may be responsible for the barbaric crimes against humanity through colonialism, slavery, the Holocaust, among other historical atrocities. It is only through our willingness to confront the demon in us that we become willing to stop demonizing and dehumanizing the other.

Freire: I agree, Donaldo. You see, for me it is far more important to study the interrelationship between white supremacy and dehumanization than to spend time and energy to maintain white supremacy through the enactment of a pseudoscience that attempts to prove black inferiority dislodged from the sociocultural conditions that may, in fact, hinder normal intellectual development. For instance, the ignorance laws that made it a crime for slaves to learn how to read and write certainly represent a socially constructed context for lack of reading ability. You cannot isolate in a scientific study the genes that seemingly are responsible for black inferior intellectual capacity while ignoring the material conditions that adversely affect cognitive and intellectual development. What is needed is not yet another study like *The Bell Curve* designed to rationalize the further abandonment of blacks. What is needed is the courage to transcend the deficit orientation supported by a suspect and racist scholarship hidden under the guise of scientism, so we can move beyond the pipe dream of a democratic education and create the reality. However, in order to make education democratic, we must simultaneously make the society within which it exists democratic as well. We cannot speak of democracy while promoting racist policies.

Macedo: Well put. Democracy in a racist society is an oxymoron.

Freire: Exactly. Thus, the humanization and the democratization of society must imply the necessary transformation of an oppressive and unjust apparatus that guides and shapes society. Since racism is a form of oppression, you can never achieve any substantive humanization by accommodating to racist structures. For me, there can never be any humanistic dimension in oppression, nor is there dehumanization in true liberation. The fact that blacks in the United States continue to be dehumanized . . . their liberation from slavery is compromised as indicated in W. E. B. DuBois' pronouncements. In order to maintain new forms of slavery, the dominant white class must attempt to eliminate blacks' capacity to think. An attempt such as this can be characterized as nothing less than an aggression against nature and against humanity. It is for this reason that authors such as Murray and Hernstein have so attempted, with technology and "science" at their disposal to generate dubious studies like those published in *The Bell Curve*.

Donaldo, when I am confronted with the arguments in *The Bell Curve*, I say strongly and loudly that we should not respect these arguments scientifically or humanistically.

Macedo: The near euphoric embracing of the debate generated by *The Bell Curve* puts your reaction against its racist propositions in the minority. In fact, *The Bell Curve* has been embraced not only by right-wing ideologues who had been impatiently waiting for science to legitimize their racism, it also has been embraced willfully by the media, which gave many authors space to shape and define the agenda on race issues in the United States. Even when the media would contest the racist propositions presented in *The Bell Curve* it nonetheless facilitated wide dissemination of these propositions which, in turn, reinforced the racist fabric of our society that is presently launching frontal attacks on affirmative action and immigrants. As David Duke, a presidential candidate in 1992, put it, "America is being invaded by hordes of dusty third-world peoples, and with each passing hour our economic well-being, cultural heritage, freedom and racial roots are being battered into oblivion."[10] One could argue that David Duke represents the fringe, but I find little substantive difference between the unveiled racism of David Duke and the scientifically veiled racism of Charles Murray and Richard Hernstein. In fact, one could easily consider Charles Murray as a David Duke in academic regalia. Given that a major portion of the data used to provide the basis for the main arguments in *The Bell Curve* was funded by the Pioneer Fund, an organization with a long history of association with Nazi groups, and the fact that Murray in his youth flirted with the burning of the cross [the book], should have been a wake-up call for those who profess to combat racism. Instead, Charles Murray has appeared in all major media outlets from conservative to the so-called liberal media such as *Nightline,* MacNeil/Lehrer, *All Things Considered,* the *New York Times Book Review,* to mention only a few. The question remains as to whether or not the media would give an antiracist book that indicts our racist society equal time. Given our society's preponderance to oppose an open debate concerning our ethical posture concerning the *Enola Gay* exhibition and given the marginalization of major dissident scholars like Noam Chomsky, even though he is considered the most influential intellectual alive in the world today, we can easily understand the celebration of questionable scholars such as Charles Murray and society's complicity with his racist tirades. Although on the surface, it may be hard to comprehend that our so-called democratic society is obviously in complicity with racism, upon further analysis it becomes less difficult to unveil the racist structures that continually debilitate our ever more fragile democracy, as demonstrated by John Sedgwick, who writes:

> [they] shouldn't be hard to find, in a country where blacks are far more likely than whites to grow up poor, fatherless, malnourished, badly educated, and victimized by crime and drugs. Then there is the matter of racism in America, which, like bloodstains on the hands of Lady MacBeth, cannot be washed away."[11]

Richard Hernstein and Charles Murray's book *The Bell Curve* represents the bloodstain of American racism. It cannot be washed away without the total transformation of the present oppressive racist structures that characterize our democracy in crisis.

NOTES

1. Albert Memmi, *The Colonizer and the Colonized* (Boston: Beacon Press, 1991), p. 74.
2. Ibid., p. 76.
3. Ibid., p. 70.
4. Ibid., p. 71.
5. Renato Constantino, *Neocolonial Identity and Counter-Consciousness* (London: Merlin Press, 1978), p. 66.
6. Steven Fraser (ed.), *The Bell Curve Wars: Race, Intelligence, and the Future of America* (New York: Basic Books, 1995), p. 1.
7. Derrick Jacson, " Reconstruction Part Two," *Boston Globe*, July 5, 1995.
8. Howard Zinn, *A Peoples' History of the United States* (New York: Harper Perennial, 1990), p. 8.
9. J. W. Gibson, *The Perfect War* (New York: Vintage Books, 1988), pp. 202-203.
10. David Nyhan, "David Duke sent 'em a Scare But Now He Faces the Old Pro," *Boston Globe*, October 24, 1991, p. 13.
11. John Sedgwick, "Inside the Pioneer Fund," in R. Jacoby and N. Glauberman (eds.), *The Bell Curve Debate* (New York: Random House, 1995).

CHAPTER 4

INSURGENT MULTICULTURALISM
A Dialogue with Henry Giroux

Most whites, some despite involvements in protests, do believe in "freedom of democracy", and they fight to make the ideals of the Constitution an empirical reality for all. . . . But it never dawns on these do-gooders that what is wrong with America is not its failure to make the Constitution a reality for all, but rather its belief that persons can affirm whiteness and humanity at the same time. This country was founded for whites and everything that has happened in it has emerged from the white perspective. . . . What we need is the deconstruction of whiteness [white supremacy], which is the source of human misery in the world.

—James Cone[1]

In this dialogue with Henry Giroux, we demonstrate that, as old borders and zones of cultural difference become more porous or eventually collapse, questions of culture increasingly become dominant; cultural traditions once self-confidently secure in the modernist discourse of progress, universalism, and objectivism are now interrogated as ideological beachheads used to police and contain subordinate groups, oppositional discourses and dissenting social movements. Struggles over the academic canon, the conflict over Multiculturalism, and the battle for either extending or containing the rights of new social groups dominate the current political and ideological landscape. What is at stake in these struggles far exceeds the particular interests that structure any one of them or the specific terrains in which they are subject to debate, whether they be the academy, the arts, schools, or other spheres of public life. Underlying the proliferation of these diverse and various battles is a deeper conflict over the relationship between democracy and culture, on the one hand, and identity and the politics of representation, on the other.

Central to this debate is an attempt to articulate the relationship among identity, culture, and democracy in a new way. For the left, this has generally meant launching an assault on monumentalist views of Western culture, a one-dimensional Eurocentric academic canon, the autonomous subject as the sovereign source of truth, and forms of high culture that maintain sexist, racist, homophobic, and class-specific relations of domination. More specifically, the challenges raised by feminism, postmodernism, and postcolonialism have contributed to a redefinition of cultural politics that addresses representational practices in terms that analyze not only their discursive power to construct common sense, textual authority, and particular social and racial formations, but also how institutions shape and regulate different expressions of culture. In this chapter, we point out that the central challenges for educators and other cultural workers attempting to address the problems is to redefine the relationship between culture and politics in order to deepen and extend the basis for transformative and emancipatory practice. As part of such a challenge, the political side of culture must be given primacy as an act of resistance and transformation by addressing issues of difference, identify, and textuality within rather than outside of the problematics of power, agency, and history. The urgent issue here is to link the politics of culture to the practice of a substantive democracy.

Bartolomé: Against the backdrop of the present "cultural wars" many progressive and liberal educators have embraced multicultural education as a means to respond both to the constant attack by conservative and reactionary educators and to develop a more inclusive pedagogy whereby issues of race, gender, ethnicity, language, and class cease to occupy a marginal position in the curriculum. In the process of reorienting the curriculum so as to address the pressing issues both progressive and liberal educators have, again, relied on the work of Paulo Freire, your work, and the work of other critical educators in their attempt to understand what it means to educate students for a less Eurocentric and more multicultural society. However, many multicultural educators with good intentions have fallen far too short of the challenge that gives primacy to the political side of culture as they embrace a form of multicultural education that is narrowly focused on diversity and tolerance. As such, your requirements to address issues of difference within the problematics of power, agency, and history are often not incorporated in a substantive way in most multicultural education programs. Can you speak about the absence of a substantive cultural democracy in the present multicultural debate?

Giroux: What seems to characterize the current moment in multicultural pedagogy is very different from what we saw when we met Paulo Freire in the early 1980s. At that time, the debate about the politics of difference was firmly situated in a long tradition of political struggle. That is, the issue of culture was linked to the ways in which culture deployed power and was deployed within iniquitous relations of power. Issues regarding identity, the politics of textuality, or adding courses to the curricula were not divorced from broader public discourses dealing with issues of struggle, power, and the redistribution of resources. This reassertion of the political was one of the characteristics that Freire brought to the dialogue when we first met him in the early 1980s. On a personal level, Paulo lived out and exhibited an enormous sense of commitment in his concern with linking pedagogical practices to political projects that addressed human suffering, misery, and oppression. It was impossible to take Paulo Freire's work seriously and not come to grips with the enormous challenge of what it meant to make the pedagogical more political and the political more pedagogical. For many of us, it was precisely this reaffirmation of the link among pedagogy, politics, culture, and social justice that allowed us to move away from an exclusive concern with class politics to a broader project that understood how class was lived out through the modalities of race, gender, and sexual orientation. Although, Paulo's early work was understandably rooted in an almost exclusive concern with class, many of us realized that it had theoretical shortcomings in dealing with the central issues shaping the multicultural debate. In part, Paulo realized this as well and moved away from an exclusive focus on class very quickly in the 1980s. At that time, many of us began to expand the notion of social justice to include a discourse about racial justice. That is, justice could not be taken up solely in terms of the ownership of the means of production, or strictly around questions of labor or the division of wealth. These were very important issues, but they excluded fundamental questions about racism, colonialism, and the workings of the racial state. But in amplifying the discourse of domination, we did not simply focus on the construction of identities, or the reading of texts so as to affirm particular identities or sexual orientations. We also tried to link the construction of social identities with a broader discourse of critical citizenship and radical democracy. Many of us had read Antonio Gramsci, Louis Althusser, Pierre Bourdieu, and Stanley Aronowitz and were engaging what was then referred to as the "crisis of materialism." This shift away from economism paved the way theoretically for us to begin to address the vexing legacy of colonialism and monoculturalism, white privilege, the struggle over meaning and representation, and the implications these might have for educational reform and radical pedagogy. But this shift in our thinking had its roots in the historical legacy of the sixties, and provided a theoretical and political framework for trying to understand the struggles identified around multiculturalism as extensions of the civil rights struggles of the 1960s. Multicultural education in this sense was about the making and unmaking of contexts where cultural difference signified sites of contestation and the politics of difference were always about relations of power and the opening up of diverse public spaces of translation and transformation. Pedagogically this suggested teaching students to interrogate how culture is regulated to eliminate difference, to include and exclude particular groups organized through the modalities of class, gender, and racial privilege, and how whiteness has been historically privileged under such circumstances. A multicultural pedagogy also offered students the opportunity to address how racial stereotypes were constructed within the media and how the dynamics of racial coding operated as part of a public pedagogy in a variety of cultural sites. It was also very important to introduce students to the legacy of antiracist struggles that had gone on over the last 300 years and to point to the gains that have emerged as a result of such struggles. For many activists, the focus on whiteness provided new pedagogical opportunities to raise issues about the very nature of the pedagogical process in terms of the authority wielded by teachers, the social locations they occupied, the partiality of their own discourses, and what it meant to problematize the subject positions from which such teachers offered up their own enunciations and particular discourses. Of course, many educators including Paulo Freire had been doing this for years, but certain critics seemed to forget this when they discovered again the importance of such pedagogical practices and claimed them as part of the disciplinary territory of feminist pedagogy, an unfortunately divisive and bogus claim.

Bartolomé: Many of these feminists have waged an attack against radical pedagogy by elevating the notion of the personal to the point of practically eliminating the political. They eliminate talk about teacher location, for instance, but never talk about what they are against in terms of particular forms of domination. Or they write profusely about creating safety zones in classrooms, or creating what has been termed comfort zones. This is what concerns me because even some progressive and liberal educators, including this particular brand of feminist pedagogy disarticulate the political from the pedagogical by trying to create a feel-good comfort zone where issues of tolerance are taken up. Meaning, if you evoke critique, you may create a tense situation whereby the comfort zone disappears or you are accused of simply exercising a form of patriarchy. This notion of comfort zone, feel-good pedagogy, is a process that even progressive thinkers, and many progressive educators know often use so as to eclipse the possibility of the political engagement that you're talking about. How can you explain that many liberals and feminists that have a progressive political posture would basically end up displacing the political from the pedagogical projects?

Giroux: I think what often goes on here is that the notion of the political literally collapse into the notion of subjective, and hence, in many ways dismantle those critical discourses that unsettle, disturb, or break into common sense. As Homi Bhabha puts it, these languages are seen as either dangerous or too traumatic. In other words, politics in this discourse is subsumed under middle-class therapy, and the personal totally envelops the political, transforming it into a risk-free zone of biographical discourses that suggests that experience somehow speaks for itself and is a transparent window on the world or guarantees a certain political purity. This is more than an act of bad faith, it also represents a rampant form of anti-intellectualism. Any discourse that demands something other than consensus, the willingness to grapple with complexities that spurn binaristic thinking, or is willing to assume the position of the "other" is seen as a violation of civility, a rupturing of a kind of alleged universal middle-class aesthetic. Critical engaged attempts to recover subjugated traditions, histories, and experience appear particularly dangerous and threatening to some white, middle-class teachers and students. In part, because these critical traditions that push against the grain often call into question both the identities and privileges enjoyed by such teachers and students. But these critical traditions also suggests that the bourgeois notion of tolerance—a theoretical prop for the comfort-zone argument—not only has little to do with antiracist struggles but actually helps to perpetuate them. What I am getting at is that for many liberals, the appeal to tolerance allows them to keep in place, or should I say to hide in the shadows, their own sense of privilege while simultaneously making it appear that they are addressing the issue of cultural difference. For many of these educators, the only way to enter into the debate about cultural difference is to situate the "alleged" others within a discourse of mutual respect, a discourse that sets the limits to what the dominant class can tolerate or find acceptable. For example, respect is often the price of the ticket that the other pays if he or she is willing to assimilate into the dominant culture, stop speaking in his or her native language, and never link difference to issues of power. But if you suggest that tolerance provides the ideological mask to hide their own privileges because it has nothing to say about structures of power and leaves institutional structures intact, it becomes clear that tolerance and the call for consensus is always produced through a process of exclusion that benefits those who have power, those who are comfortable in the very relations of power that are now being called into question. Hence, such a discourse threatens not only the dominant classes own sense of identity, but their relationship to the world around them. So, I think at one level any pedagogy that in some way unsettles the comfortable nature of established identities contains the possibility for becoming a threat to both teachers and students, especially those who operate from a position of privilege and power. I also think that it is very difficult for many students, especially those who are privileged by virtue of race, class, and gender to take up the question of politics because it always suggests something about the political nature of their own sense of agency and social responsibility that many of them may not want to deal with. For example, critical educators might suggest that to take multiculturalism seriously means addressing such important issues as the militarization of inner-city schools, the shrinking of city services for the urban poor, a restructured economy that decimates the employment possibilities of poor black and brown people, and a growing prison-industrial complex which not only incarcerates disproportionate numbers of black youth but forces many states such as California and Maryland to spend more on prison maintenance and growth than on higher education. Many middle-class people don't want to hear about these issues, because they are unsettling, and rightly so. These issues make multiculturalism more than adding new books to the curricula or appropriating writers of color. They suggests that pedagogy always emerges out of concrete projects in the real world and have an ethical referent. Multiculturalist pedagogy in this sense is about linking the academy with the world outside of its borders, and at the very least suggest entering into areas of concern that link pedagogy and the dynamics of race as it works through daily life. This type of pedagogy also pushes against the grain of a dominant strand in American life, which privatizes everything. Citizenship has become an utterly privatized affair, and can be seen in the call not only for the privatizing of public services but also in the reduction of social agency to the act of consuming. The logic of corporate culture becomes more pervasive in the United States and other parts of the world, multiculturalism runs the risk of becoming nothing more than diversity management, new outlets for markets and consumer identities. A kind of Benetton multiculturalism. This type of public pedagogy poses a real threat to democracy. Young people, especially, are constantly fed the myth that to be an agent in the world is to be a consumer rather than a citizen activist.

Bartolomé: But the threat doesn't only come from corporate culture. It also comes from a kind of methodology madness that has a long tradition in American education, whether it be a hangover from empiricism, Social Darwinism, or simply the scientific management movement.

Giroux: I agree. It is very important to stress that in many schools of education, pedagogy is viewed as a technical practice rather than the outcome of political and social struggles. Rather than seeing pedagogy as a political and ethical practice, students often experience the pedagogical as a method, a form of learning that prescribes, dictates, but never really critically engages them to ask tough questions, take risks, and commit themselves as public intellectuals. This is the underlying ideology of the comfort-free-zone argument, but as you have suggested can only be understood within a number of historically situated traditions such as scientific management. The latter movement was designed to control workers, to reduce them to cogs in the productive apparatus. It is a lethal practice and in its various educational mutations; it still functions to deskill, disempower, and uneducate. The message is clear: Don't ask me to take a chance, interrogate my own privileges, learn how to be a critical agent, or be willing to appropriate alternative discourses and subject positions. I don't have a lot of sympathy with this position. I realize that there are many reasons for occupying it, but it is used in the current historical conjuncture as a weapon of power to shut down criticism and any form of critical pedagogy.

Bartolomé: But, the comfort-zone argument not only displaces the possibility of discussing difficult and complex issues, it also serves to reproduce a kind of privileged middle-class reality. The vast majority of inner-city students don't have a comfort zone much less the right to demand that the teacher must guarantee such comfort zones in the classroom.

Giroux: The underlying class nature of this position is all too clear when you look at what it protects and the conditions under which it becomes possible. And, of course, one of those conditions is exclud-ing those voices that would challenge this type of psychobabble and maintaining the inequalities that provoke such challenges in the first place.

Bartolomé: The blindness to which you refer shows that even by basically rejecting some forms of traditional pedagogics, these teach-ers who are now under the umbrella of progressive education are basi-cally enslaved to the individualistic posture which is part of the dominant ideology. So, by doing away with the political, they have no tools to politically understand how individualism is, in fact, making them a prey of the traditional pedagogy that they are in the process of rejecting. On the other hand, they produce and reproduce many of those traditional values that they proclaim to abandon as they embrace multiculturalism.

Giroux: In this case, multiculturalism simply becomes a code word for cultural diversity, a reformist form of pluralism in which cul-tural difference is reduced to the attribute of equal respect and dis-tinctly separated cultural traditions. Within this discourse there is no recognition that cultural locations are, as Homi Bhabha puts it "nego-tiated in a cross-boundary process" and that the the politics of multi-culturalism is not simply about the proliferation of diverse cultures, but that difference becomes a problem when "something is being challenged about power or authority."[2] Within the discourse of plural-ism, identities are about the search for roots, not about how identities mutate, change, and hybridize. All to often, identities remain isolated and static rather than dynamic and diasporic. Similarly, there is no recognition here of the unequal development of social groups within historical legacies of oppression, nor is there a call to open up institu-tional space and distribute power and resources so that the discourse of respect and recognition translates into parity and economic justice. Pluralism does not challenge linear histories or dominant cultural totalities, it simply reaffirms them as the referent for acknowledging other cultural groups who may be offered some crumbs to join the elite club. There is no discussion in the pluralism model that suggests that questions of cultural difference entail a rearticulation of the very meaning of citizenship, nation formation as the construction of "the people." This is not meant to suggest that caring and empathy, stalwarts of the liberal pedagogical model, are irrelevant. However, we have to be vigilant about pedagogical approaches that endorse notions of caring that either prevent the engagement of pertinent political issues at work in multicultural education or serve to produce other forms of "benevolent" oppression. Put differently, we need to mediate any notion of caring and empathy through the related issues of solidarity and politics. What does it mean for teachers and students to think of the concept of identity in new ways, to think at the limit regarding the issue of identity? What is the political importance of the notion of identity in relation to the central questions of agency and politics? How can we address the issue of identity as a strategic and positional concept rather than think of it in essentialized or fixed terms? Stuart Hall has argued that identities are less about the issue of origins—who we are or where we came from—and more about the issue of identifications. The issue of identifications raises another set of questions about how subject positions are represented, about how identities are shaped and what form they might take. Hall's emphasis is on engaging identity as a question of appropriation and use, and raises important questions regarding how are identities are fashioned within the resources of culture, language, history, and machineries of power. Caring represents a specific discourse that is produced within particular ideologies and social practices. The issue here is how does such a discursive formation address the relationship between difference and power within specific historical and institutional sites? What subject positions are constructed through its forms of address? How does it justify some subject positions and not others? How does it articulate between the personal and social, the private and the public? How might a pedagogy of caring encourage certain identifications while always raising questions that unsettle those notions of identity that are static and ideologically oppressive.

Identity or the politics of difference should not be policed. It should be pluralized, opened up, connected to the resources of history, linked to global contexts, and expanded in order to provide the economic, social, and cultural opportunities for people to become agents both individually and collectively—enabling them to become the subjects rather than the objects of history.

Bartolomé: But this notion of caring that you are talking about is problematic because in seemingly creating a comfort zone under the pretext of caring, they sloganize that we need to love our students, even though they don't critique the very structures that generate devaluations of subordinated students. By not interrogating the dominant social order, those teachers become complicitous with the very structure that basically produces the human misery to which they object. In other words, by not being willing to deconstruct the very ideology and by promoting a pedagogy of caring only, they end up basically arguing for a comfort zone restricted to the classroom only. This position constitutes what Paulo Freire calls an entrapment pedagogy. It is also a process through which middle-class teachers deal with their own class guilt under the guise of caring for these students either by promoting a false notion of social promotion that deskills students and by indulging them in an overcelebrating of self that could lead to a level of narcissism. It think that the so-called caring pedagogy needs to be retaken theoretically. That is why these educators avoid theory—they avoid theory because theory would force them to look critically at those forces that are really producing the conditions that produce human misery.

Giroux: I am not supporting a notion of caring that promotes this type of abuse and escapism. On the contrary, I am simply arguing that all forms of caring cannot be reduced to this ideological position. Caring for students matters, and I think it is essential that any decent pedagogy make it a condition for becoming a teacher. Teachers who hate kids are not exactly models for critical pedagogy, but at the same time caring as an ideological construct is a contested terrain, and I am suggesting that we need to appropriate those critical elements in a pedagogy of caring that do not lend themselves to the kind of narcissism you are talking about. For example, the work of a feminist such as Sharon Welch embodies what I am talking about. Her notion of caring is linked to the issue of social justice, not to expanding the level of one's comfort zone.

Bartolomé: I think that approach still runs the risk of becoming a form of therapy. It's again a process that merely psychologizes.

Giroux: There are multiple entries into linking pedagogy with the politics of experience that can avoid what you call psychologizing. One can begin to excavate student experiences by connecting them with popular culture, with elements of high culture, or with a whole range of other texts. Affirming such experiences as part of a pedagogy of critical engagement means honoring the experiences that people use to make their worlds meaningful and their identities functional. This suggests a pedagogy that cares about who students are and where they come from, and where they are going as these experiences get mobilized and used to narrate their identities and relationship to the world. If educators only affirmed these experiences, or treated them as if they were static and fixed, we would fall into the trap that a lot of theorists replicate under the heading of a pedagogy of caring. But in this triangulation of identification, mediation, and experience there is more than just intimacy and affirmation, there is also the discourse of responsibility and critical engagement. Knowledge in this case is not overly dependent on the intersubjective; it is also concerned with issues of power and control over the material conditions for the production of knowledge and how the latter affect what might count as an argument, what counts as viable knowledge and reliable evidence. The issue is to politicize such experience rather than simply affirm it. And by politicizing it, I mean understanding its limitations, its connections to other discourses, and its complicity as well as resistance with particular forms of domination. Moreover, I think any discourse of caring that is simply concerned about how we talk about issues rather than how we both understand and change them is ultimately part of a domineering subjectivity that stands in the way of progressive change. This kind of pedagogy suffers from three important constraints. First, it treats students as if they were nothing more than bundles of needs whose greatest desire is to be affirmed and satisfied, and in doing so substitutes a therapeutic discourse for a discourse of social responsibility and critical engagement. Second, by focusing on issues of experience and intimacy, it has no way of engaging networks of institutional power relations that cause human oppression. Third, it is a me-centered discourse in which the quest for meaning supersedes the search for justice, particularly class and racial justice. We see instances of this work in a great deal of critical pedagogy that actually prides itself on this type of naval-gazing politics. I am thinking in particular of the work of Jane Tompkins, Carol Gilligan, and the authors of *Woman's Ways of Knowing*. I think any radical pedagogy that matters needs to make experience the object of critical analysis, subject it to the lens of critical theory, and break into its notions of common sense. The claim to authenticating experience offers no political guarantees, but is an important starting point to begin any critical pedagogical intervention. I mean, you can begin with the experience and then theoretically deconstruct that experience so that experience then becomes problematic and capable of doing the work of some form of self and social examination.

Bartolomé: This also involves the historicizing of experience.

Giroux: I think experience needs to be historicized. Experience is not simply a social construction but also a historical construction, though I don't think this means reading experience against some discourse of authentic origins as much as it suggests tracing the routes rather than roots that such experience takes. In this discourse, experience becomes the stuff of subjugated memories, traces of memory that are often considered dangerous to dominant ideologies, narrative imaginings that are capable of rewriting the past and challenging the present. I think experience in these terms is about identity formation, and raises serious issues about how we are positioned within particular experiences, how such experiences are negotiated, and in some cases how they can be resisted or unlearned. We need to address this notion of experience seriously and not confuse it with a solipsistic pedagogy of caring.

Bartolomé: You mentioned before the infusion of ethics and the need for the development of an ethical posture in pedagogy. While ethics is of paramount importance, the curricula in schools of education presently do not provide pedagogical opportunities for students to struggle and understand the ethical role in teaching and learning. For instance, while students are required to take courses in statistics, assessment, and other technical bodies of knowledge, there are, to my knowledge, no schools which require students to take courses on ethics as part of their core requirements. The same applies to ideology.

Giroux: Education always presupposes a vision of the future in its introduction to, preparation for, and legitimation of particular forms of social life. In other words, it is a deeply embedded moral practice. The implications of this understanding is that educators must make visible the moral visions and social ethics that provide their referents for justifying a particular form of pedagogical practice. As a form of provocation and challenge, pedagogy is rooted in an ethical-political vision that attempts to take people beyond the world they already know and as such should be accountable for the ideologies that motivate such visions, the practices they legitimate, and the consequences to which they point. The point here is that how we educate students, if such an education is to be about more than training, needs to emphasize a discourse of ethics, vision, and politics over a discourse of methods and verification. Any decent school of education should provide the theoretical, political, and social contexts from which to organize the energies of a diverse number of moral visions. I am not suggesting that schools of education impose a moral vision on students, but that they make students aware that if schools of education are to play a productive role in reclaiming the legacy of public schools as democratic public spheres, they need to provide students with the ethical discourses that enable them be accountable for how they wield authority and power, to learn how to take risks, awaken the moral and civic consciousness of young people, and interrogate the consequences of their own institutionally based pedagogical practices. Schools of education it seems to me have a responsibility to educate young people about what it means to defend education as a public good, and this suggests teaching students to take seriously what it means for authority to work in the interests of expanding the capacity of students to be critical and active citizens rather than simply consuming subjects.

Bartolomé: Well, the notion of doing away with authority is the source of confusion among many educators. Authority exists by the fact that the teacher has mastery over a particular body of knowledge. However, having authority through the knowledge of one's field of specialization, does not mean teaching this body of knowledge in an authoritarian fashion. Even when teachers propose to give away their authority so as to become mere facilitators, they are being disingenuous. In fact, it is a false notion because you really don't give up your authority. You pretend to give it away. And this is part of the issue that Paulo discusses concerning the difference of teachers and facilitators. Teachers as facilitators pretend to exercise no authority over students, which, is, in fact, false. The teacher still grades, selects materials, decides on major issues to cover, etc. He or she is not given up that authority. I think, how do you reconfigure the authority, how do you problematize this?

Giroux: There is a general confusion among a number of educators on the left who suggest that authority and authoritarianism are the same thing. There is a certain type of displacement that takes place in this type of argument, a displacement that is characterized by a retreat from politics and political responsibility. The essential question is how can authority be legitimated, used, and problematized in order to provide the conditions for students and others to learn how to exercise authority in the interest of both challenging it and using it to democratize social relations. That is, how can teacher authority be used to provide the resources, institutional spaces, social relations, and knowledge that can be critically appropriated by students to expand their capacities to be social actors, critical subjects of history. These are the kinds of questions we have to deal with in addressing the relationship between authority and politics. I think the other side of this issue is that the question of authority also has to become instrumental in establishing the conditions for not only making knowledge the object of social criticisms but also for examining the location and politics of those who are institutionally sanctioned to wield the power of authority. The fact of the matter is that pedagogical work takes place in institutions grounded in hierarchical forms of power, and the authority we assume within such relations should be open to examination by students as well as other teachers. But, of course, the point here is that academics cannot renounce their intellectual authority and the discourses they produce, and should remember that students only negotiate rather than absorb those discursive maps. What we can do as educators is make the projects that drive the knowledge, values, and needs we present as open as possible for students to negotiate and critically engage; hence, authority can be used to promote critique, reflexiveness, contingency, and multiple forms of engagement. Schools should always been seen as sites of unequal struggles over power rather than as binaristic inside/outside relations. This is a more dialectical model for taking up the importance of authority and the kinds of responsibilities it entails politically and ethically. I think that Stuart Hall is very insightful in suggesting that authority must be understood within the projects and social formations it emerges out of and in part legitimates and contests. At its best, authority is central to any political project in which pedagogy can be used to "address the central, urgent and disturbing questions of a society in the most rigorous intellectual way we have available." Authority provides the referent and conditions for allowing such practices to be developed by both teachers and students.

Bartolomé: I agree.

Giroux: But I want to go back to something I have just said and extend the argument somewhat because of the importance of the issue. It is crucial to acknowledge that authority also raises serious strategic questions about dealing with institutional constraints and power. How can critical educators use their power to work against the very institutions that provide such power in the first place? This is a complex issue that points to the multifaceted ways in which authority becomes operative. How can critical educators have one foot in and one foot out of dominant institutional spaces so as to be able to exercise authority as a tool for change against these very institutions that make such authority possible? Educators need to make their systems of meaning, and the inclusions and exclusions that shape them, both visible and available for critical engagement. Of course, this suggests opening a theoretical space that may be difficult to defend, one that reveals the partiality of our arguments, but this is precisely what authority should do—offer a reflexive review of its own projects, history, and presuppositions, and make a case for defending such practices as part of a broader defense of the relationship between knowledge and commitment. At the same time, this approach to authority recognizes that such authority is crucial in contesting the needs, ideas, ideologies, and values that students bring to the class-room. Authority is not simply unsettling because of the power it wields; it is unsettling because it should be used to get teachers and students to rethink the meaning of what they know, how they act, and how they relate to the world around them. This is not a small matter and indicates how banal and utterly simplistic some arguments can be when they simply denounce all authority as a form of authoritari-anism. The capacities for self-reflection, mastering different forms of knowledge, inhabiting different desiring maps, struggling over partic-ular forms of identification always speak to the conditions available for agency to develop and the forms of authority at work in opening up or closing down such opportunities for different individuals and groups. To renounce authority is to abandon politics itself and what it means to struggle over those spaces and pedagogical relations that encourage students to consider their own positions within particular social discourses, historical locations, the practical relations of every-day life, and address the implications of the latter for deploying authority and power in shaping their own lives. Because authority is always linked to questions of power, it is inextricably linked to issues regarding citizenship (who is included and who is not), democracy (who decides what it means and how it is implemented), and agency (who has the power to shape everyday life and under what circum-stances do people assume such a role).

Bartolomé: What is the relationship between literacy and Multi-culturalism? How can we theorize such a relationship in light of the current struggle of right-wing groups such as the English First move-ment?

Giroux: The struggle over literacy is fundamentally about the abil-ity of people to narrate their own histories and experiences within a politics of cultural difference and recognition. It suggests not only that culture is pluralized and is shaped through multiple languages, it also points to the need for people to become border crossers and to learn how to negotiate cultural differences through referents other than those sanctioned by dominant discourses. Clearly, the struggle over language, in part, is about the battle over identities and the ability of those who are considered marginal, different, and other to speak in their own terms. But the notion of multiple literacies also offers the opportunity for students to produce new cultures out of old ones, to bring together old traditions and fashion them into new and vibrant cultural forms. Literacy when pluralized offers the opportunity to create multiple cultural forms, to create a society that as Stuart Hall argues has been mongrelized by the variety of peoples who locate themselves within multiple groups, relationships, languages, and communities. Multiple literacy speaks to a kind of citizenship that is open and democratic rather than a citizenship that creates a fortress against difference and diversity. Literacy is a productive force and regulatory power, but at the same time "being literate," while linked to the acquisition of agency, learning how to be responsible to oneself within the play of discourse, does not guarantee anything. One can be literate and be a fascist. Literacy is a precondition for agency, but it does not provide or sanction any political guarantees. At its best, as Homi Bhabha, has pointed out, literacy is not about competence, it is about "intervention, the possibility of interpretation as intervention, as interrogation, as relocation, as revision."[3] I think it is this political and pedagogical aspect of literacy and its link to the production of democratic identities, representations, and social relations that we need to pay more attention to in schools of education. The call for multiple literacies is really about providing the pedagogical conditions and resources for students to produce their own readings, assume responsibility for their enunciations and cultural productions, and learn how to read differently so as to pluralize the meaning of citizenship and cultural membership.

Bartolomé: What are some of the most important threats undermining a radical multiculturalism in the academy today?

Giroux: If the academy is to assume a central role in contesting racial injustice, class hierarchies, and the politics of exclusion, progressive academics will have to challenge those post-structuralist and postmodern versions of multicultural textualism that reduce culture to the logic of signification. As Larry Grossberg points out, culture must not be equated with the domain of meaning and representation, but rather addressed as "both a form of discursive practice and an analysis of institutional conditions."[4] Equally important to politically viable academic work is the recognition that the struggle over culture is not a substitute for some kind of "real" or "concrete" form of politics, but a crucial "site of the production and struggle over power—where power is understood not necessarily in the form of domination"[5] but as a productive and mediating force for the making and remaking of diverse and interconnected social, political, and economic contexts that make up daily life. As citizenship becomes increasingly privatized and students are increasingly educated to become consuming subjects rather than critical social subjects, it becomes all the more imperative for educators to rethink how the educational force of the culture works to both secure and resist particular identities and values. In opposition to born-again multiculturalists such as Nathan Glazer (who declares that "we are all multiculturalists now"), progressive educators can foreground the importance of critical work in higher education as part of a broader radical democratic project to recover and rethink the ways in which culture is related to power and how and where it functions both symbolically and institutionally as an educational, political, and economic force that refuses to live with difference or simply manage it as part of the deadly logic of assimilation and control.

As more and more young people face a world of increasing poverty, unemployment, and diminished social opportunities, those of us in education can struggle to vindicate the crucial connection between culture and politics in defending higher education as an essential democratic public sphere dedicated to providing students with the knowledge, skills, and values they will need to address some of the most urgent questions of our time. But if addressing multiculturalism as a form of cultural politics within the university is to become a meaningful pedagogical practice, academics will have to reevaluate the relationship between culture and power as a starting point for bearing witness to the ethical and political dilemmas that connect the university to other spheres within the broader social landscape. In doing so, we need to become more attentive to how multicultural politics gets worked out in urban spaces and public spheres that are currently experiencing the full force of the right-wing attack on culture and racial difference. It is no longer possible for academics to make a claim to a radical politics of multiculturalism by defining it merely as a set of intellectual options and curriculum imperatives. Academic multiculturalism must also examine actual struggles taking place in the name of cultural difference within institutional sites and cultural formations that bear the brunt of dominant machineries of power designed to exclude, contain, or disadvantage the oppressed. The institutional and cultural spheres bearing the brunt of the racialization of the social order are increasingly located in the public schools, in the criminal justice system, in retrograde anti-immigrant policy legislation, and in the state's ongoing attempts to force welfare recipients into workfare programs.[6]

I am not suggesting that we redefine multiculturalism by moving away from issues of representation or shifting our pedagogical efforts in the interests of a democratic politics of difference away from the university. On the contrary, we need to vitalize our efforts within the university by connecting the intellectual work we do there with a greater effort to pressing public problems and social responsibilities. A radical approach to multiculturalism must address how material relations of power work to sustain structures of inequality and exploitation in the current racialization of the social order. It must ask specific questions about the forms racial domination and subordination take within the broader public culture and how their organization, operation, and effects both implicate and affect the meaning and purpose of higher education. At stake here is the need for critical educators to give meaning to the belief that academic work matters in its relationship to broader public practices and policies; and that such work holds the possibility for understanding not just how power operates in particular contexts, but also how such knowledge "will better enable people to change the context and hence the relations of power"[7] that inform the inequalities that undermine any viable notion of Multiculturalism within spheres as crucial to democracy as the public schools and higher education.

In short, I want to insist that multiculturalism is not simply an educational problem. At its roots it is about the relationship between politics and power; it's about a historical past and a living present where racist exclusions appear "calculated, brutally rational, and profitable."[8]

Bartolomé: What do you say to conservatives and liberals who argue that race is no longer a determining force in American society and therefore multiculturalism is basically outdated, or worse, reproduces a racist discourse?

Giroux: Embedded within a systemic history of black restriction, subjugation, and white privilege, the politics of racial discrimination and exclusion is still, as Supreme Court Justice Ruth Bader Ginsburg puts it, "evident in our workplaces, markets and neighborhoods."[9] One of the more compelling arguments against this color-blind notion of race has been provided by David Shipler in his new book, *A Country of Strangers*. Shipler argues powerfully that race and class are the two most powerful determinants shaping American society. After interviewing hundreds of people over a five year-period, Shipler's book bears witness to a racism that "is a bit subtler in expression, more cleverly coded in public, but essentially unchanged as one of the 'deep abiding currents' in every day life, in both the simplest and the most complex interactions of whites and blacks."[10]

Although there can be little doubt that racial progress has been achieved in many areas in the last fifty years,[11] it is also true that such progress has not been sustained. This is particularly evident in the dramatic increase in black prisoners and the growth of the prison-industrial complex, crumbling city infrastructures, segregated housing, soaring black and Latino unemployment, exorbitant school dropout rates among black and Latino youth coupled with the realities of failing schools more generally and deepening inequalities of incomes and wealth between blacks and whites.[12] Pushing against the grain of civil rights reform and racial justice are reactionary and moderate positions ranging from the extremism of right-wing skinheads and Jesse Helms-like conservatives to the moderate "color-blind" positions of liberals such as Randall Kennedy.

Bartolomé: Does this type of refusal suggest a new type of racism in the United States?

Giroux: Yes, in some ways I think it is fair to say it takes on a different register. This type of racism combines a kind of genteel academicism with the crudity of Social Darwinism and it does so through right-wing funding and the use of the dominant media. Crucial to the reemergence of this "new" racism is a cultural politics that plays a determining role in how race shapes our popular unconscious. This is evident in the widespread articles, reviews, and commentaries in the dominant media that give inordinate amounts of time and space to mainstream conservative authors, filmmakers, and critics who rail against affirmative action, black welfare mothers, and the alleged threats black youth and rap artists pose to middle-class existence. This is a racism that trades on racial panics, pits the suburbs against urban centers, and claims that white people are the real victims of identity politics.

Bartolomé: How should educators deal with this type of racial attack?

Giroux: Rather than dismiss such rampant conservatism as either indifferent to the realities of racism or deconstruct its codes to see where such language falls in on itself, educators can engage these commentaries more constructively by analyzing how they function as public discourses, how their privileged meanings work intertextually to resonate with ideologies produced in other sites, and how they serve largely to construct and legitimate racially exclusive practices, policies, and social relations. Central to such a project is the need to link a multicultural politics of representation with a representational politics in which cultural texts can be explored as examples of a racist public pedagogy, which offer students and teachers opportunities to critically engage how certain meanings carried in such texts gain the force of common sense in light of how racism is articulated in other public spheres and institutionalized sites.

Bartolomé: Are you suggesting that cultural politics can play a role within academic multiculturalism?

Giroux: Exactly. Where power becomes central to the study of cultural texts and practices, theoretical engagement with socially relevant problems can explore those wider institutional contexts and public spaces in which multicultural discourses gain their political and economic force. In order to deepen the cultural politics of multiculturalism, educators must consider addressing questions of culture, power, identity, and representation as part of a broader discourse about public pedagogy and social policy. If teaching students to interrogate cultural practices that sustain racism is a central objective of multicul-tural education, it must be addressed in ways that link such texts to the major social problems that animate public life. Texts in this instance would be analyzed as part of a "social vocabulary of culture" that points to how power names, shapes, defines, and constrains rela-tionships between the self and the other, constructs and disseminates what counts as knowledge, and produces representations that provide the context for identity formation.[13] Within this type of pedagogical approach, multiculturalism must find ways to acknowledge the politi-cal character of culture through strategies of understanding and engagement that link an antiracist and radically democratic rhetoric with strategies to transform racist institutionalized structures within and outside of the university.

At its best, academic multiculturalism should forge a connection between reading texts and reading public discourses in order to link the struggle for inclusion with relations of power in the broader soci-ety. It is precisely within the realm of a cultural politics that teachers and students develop pedagogical practices that close the gap between intellectual debate and public life not simply as a matter of relevance but as a process through which students can learn the skills and knowledge to develop informed opinions, make critical choices, and function as citizen activists. Robin D. G. Kelley provides one direction such a project might take. He insightfully argues:

> [Multiculturalism cannot ignore] how segregation strips com-munities of resources and reproduces inequality. The decline of decent-paying jobs and city services, erosion of public space, deterioration of housing stock and property values, and stark inequalities in education and health care are manifestations of investment strategies under de facto segregation. . . . [Progres-sives must address] dismantling racism, bringing oppressed populations into power and moving beyond a black/white binary that renders invisible the struggles of Latinos, Asian-Americans, Native Americans, and other survivors of racist exclusion and exploitation.[14]

I think Kelley is right on target on this issue and provides a project out of which any viable notion of multiculturalism within the university might emerge. If multiculturalism is to gain any credible force within the university, it needs to address the legacy of white racism, and move away from an identity politics and politics of textuality that divorces itself from the machineries of power and social problems that constitute the larger society. Intellectuals need to make their work meaningful by connecting what they do to broader social issues and problems. This is not a call to politicize the university or teacher work, because it is already happening. On the contrary, it is a call to make what we do matter in ways that void dogmatism and expand the possibilities for democratic public life. The times may seem indifferent for such a task, but any alternative does not augur well for democracy in this country.

NOTES

1. James Cone, cited in bell hooks, *Killing Rage: Ending Racism* (New York: Henry Holt and Company, 1995), p. 149.

2. Cited in Gary Olson and Lynn Worsham, "Staging the Politics of Difference: Homi Bhabha's Critical Literacy," *Journal of Composition Theory* 18, no. 3 (1998), p. 362.

3. Ibid.

4. Lawrence Grossberg, "Cultural Studies: What's in a Name?" *Bringing It All Back Home: Essays on Cultural Studies* (Durham: Duke University Press, 1997), p. 268.

5. Ibid., p. 248.

6. Manning Marable, "Beyond Color-Blindness," *The Nation* (December 14, 1998), p. 31.

7. Lawrence Grossberg, "Cultural Studies: What's in a Name?," pp. 252-253.

8. David Theo Goldberg, *Racist Culture* (Cambridge, MA: Basil Blackwell, 1993), p. 105.

9. Ginsberg cited in editorial, "Race On Screen and Off," *The Nation* (December 29, 1997), p. 6.

10. Shipler summarized in Jack H. Geiger, "The Real World of Race," *The Nation* (December 1, 1998), p. 27. *See also,* David Shipler, "Reflections on Race," *Tikkun* 13, no. 1 (1998), pp. 59, 78; David Shipler, *A Country of Strangers: Blacks and Whites in America* (New York: Vintage, 1998).

11. Ellen Willis argues that the two major upheavals to America's racial hierarchy have been the destruction of the Southern caste system of and the subversion of whiteness as an unquestioned norm. She also argues rightly that to dismiss

these achievements as having done little to change racist power relations insults people who have engaged in these struggles. See Ellen Willis, "The Up and Up: On the Limits of Optimism," *Transition* 7, no. 2 (1998), pp. 44-61.

12. For a compilation of figures suggesting the ongoing presence of racism in American society, see Ronald Walters, "The Criticality of Racism," *Black Scholar* 26, no. 1 (Winter 1996), pp. 2-8; A Report from the Children's Defense Fund, Yearbook 1998, *The State of America's Children* (Boston: Beacon Press, 1998).

13. Katya Gibel Azoulay, "Experience, Empathy and Strategic Essentialism," *Cultural Studies* 11, no. 1 (1997), p. 91.

14. Robin D. G. Kelley, "Integration: What's Left," *The Nation* (December 14, 1998), p. 18.

CHAPTER 5

BEYOND THE METHODS FETISH
Toward a Humanizing Pedagogy

As we discussed in chapters 1 and 2, the field of multicultural education and the education of linguistic minority students has been mostly defined by a plethora of methods designed primarily to teach tolerance. These methods not only blindly embrace the hidden (and sometimes not so opaque) assumption that the intolerable features of the "other" will be altered, reformed and, ultimately assimilated into an invisible culture of whiteness that serves as the yardstick against which cultural differences are measured. These methods also overemphasize teaching as a form of management of cultural differences while de-emphasizing learning, which is usually characterized by complexity, contradictions, and resistance. By focusing primarily on teaching methodology with respect to the education of culturally different students, even well-intentioned educators who want to give subordinated students voice fall prey to the weight of their complicity with the dominant ideology, which often remains beyond interrogation. With the exception of a handful of critical multiculturalists such as Christine Sleeter, Peter McLaren, Henry Giroux, David Goldberg, among others, most multicultural education as practice by many white liberals often refrains from deconstructing the dominant ideology that informs and shapes the asymmetrical distribution of cultural goods. These liberal educators also often fail to understand resistance as a form of cultural production that, in some real sense, gives witness to the emergence of submerged voices of subordinated students. By not understanding the critical role of cultural resistance as a learning tool and as an expression of voice, these well-intentioned liberal educators will, at best, embrace a form of charitable paternalism and, at worse, reproduce the very dominant ideological elements, they purport to eradicate through the teaching of tolerance.

In order to move beyond a mere politics of tolerance, educators will have to undergo a paradigm shift that will involve a de-emphasis on teaching methods as an end in themselves so as to fully understand how subordinated students learn in contexts characterized by economic exploitation, power asymmetries, racism, sexism, classism, and ethnic xenophobia. By refocusing on learning instead of teaching, educators will be able to develop a lucid clarity regarding the interrelationship between learning and teaching in order to realize that there is no teaching without learning and that learning ultimately determines and shapes teaching. As Paulo Freire correctly argues,

> . . . Teaching is not about transferring knowledge or contents. Nor is it an act whereby a creator-subject gives shape, style, or soul to an indecisive and complacent body. There is, in fact, no teaching without learning. . . . Socially and historically, women and men discovered that it was the process of learning that made (and makes) teaching possible. Learning in social contexts through the ages, people discovered that it was possible to develop ways, paths, and methods of teaching. To learn, then, logically precedes to teach. In other words, to teach is part of the very fabric of learning.[1]

To the extent that Paulo Freire is correct, and we believe he is, the teaching of culturally subordinated students should be preceded by a learning process that not only transforms those who learn from the "other" so as to teach the "other," but such learning provides those who want to teach with the possibility to "develop ways, paths, and methods of teaching."

Unfortunately, much of the current debate regarding the improvement of minority student academic achievement occurs at a level that treats education as a primarily technical issue.[2] For example, the historical academic underachievement of certain culturally and linguistically subordinated student populations in the United States (e.g., Mexican Americans, Native Americans, Puerto Ricans,) is perceived to be, in large part, a technical problem.[3] As such, the solution to the problem of academic underachievement tends to be constructed in technical terms dislodged from the sociocultural reality that shapes it. That is, the solution to the historical underachievement of students from subordinated cultures is often reduced to finding the "right" teaching methods, strategies, or prepackaged curricula that will work with students who do not respond to so-called regular or normal instruction.

Recent research studies have begun to identify educational programs found to be successful in working with culturally and linguistically subordinated minority student populations.[4] In addition, there has been specific interest in identifying teaching strategies that more effectively teach culturally and linguistically "different" students and other "disadvantaged" and "at risk" students.[5] Although it is important to identify useful and promising instructional programs and strategies, it is erroneous to assume that blind replication of instructional programs or teacher mastery of particular teaching methods, in and of themselves, will guarantee successful student learning, especially when we are discussing populations that historically have been mistreated and miseducated by the schools.

This focus on methods as solutions in the current literature coincides with many of our graduate students' beliefs regarding linguistic minority education improvement. As minority professors who have taught antiracist multicultural education courses at various institutions, we are consistently confronted at the beginning of each semester by students who are anxious to learn the latest teaching methods—methods that they hope will somehow magically work on minority students. Although our students are well-intentioned individuals who sincerely wish to create positive learning environments for culturally and linguistically subordinated students, they arrive with the expectation that we will provide them with easy answers in the form of specific instructional methods. That is, since they (implicitly) perceive the academic underachievement of subordinated students as a technical issue, the solutions they require are also expected to be technical in nature (e.g., specific teaching methods, instructional curricula and materials, etc.). They usually assume that: (1) they, as teachers, are fine and do not need to identify, interrogate, and change their biased beliefs and fragmented views about subordinated students; (2) schools, as institutions, are basically fair and democratic sites where all students are provided with similar, if not equal, treatment and learning conditions; and (3) children who experience academic difficulties (especially those from culturally and linguistically low-status groups) require some form of "special" instruction, since they obviously have not been able to succeed under "regular" or "normal" instructional conditions. Consequently, if nothing is basically wrong with teachers and schools, they often conclude, then linguistic minority academic underachievement is best dealt with by providing teachers with specific teaching methods that promise to be effective with culturally and linguistically subordinated students. To further complicate matters, many of our students seek *generic* teaching methods that will work with a variety of minority student populations, and they grow anxious and impatient when reminded that instruction for any group of students needs to be tailored or individualized to some extent. Some of our students appear to be seeking what María de la Luz Reyes[6]defines as a "one size fits all" instructional recipe. Reyes explains that the term refers to the assumption that instructional methods that are deemed effective for mainstream populations will benefit *all* students, no matter what their backgrounds may be. She explains that the assumption is

> similar to the "one size fits all" marketing concept that would have buyers believe that there is an average or ideal size among men and women. . . . Those who market "one size fits all" products suggest that if the article of clothing is not a good fit, the fault is not with the design of the garment, but those who are too fat, too skinny, too tall, too short, or too high-waisted.[7]

We have found that many of our students similarly believe that teaching approaches that work with one minority population should also fit another.[8] Reyes argues that educators often make this "one size fits all" assumption when discussing instructional approaches, such as process writing. For example, as Lisa Delpit[9] has convincingly argued, the process writing approach that has been blindly embraced by mostly white liberal teachers often produces a negative result with African-American students. Delpit cites one black student:

> I didn't feel she was teaching us anything. She wanted us to correct each other's papers and we were there to learn from her. She didn't teach anything, absolutely nothing. Maybe they're trying to learn what black folks knew all the time. We understand how to improvise, how to express ourselves creatively. When I'm in a classroom, I'm not looking for that, I'm looking for structure, the more formal language. Now my buddy was in a black teacher's class. And that lady was very good. She went through and explained and defined each part of the structure. This [white] teacher didn't get along with that black teacher. She said she didn't agree with her methods. But *I* don't think that white teacher *had* any methods.[10]

The above quotation is a glaring testimony that a "one size fits all" approach often does not work with the same level of effectiveness with all students across the board. Such assumptions reinforce a disarticulation between the embraced method and the social- cultural realities within which each method is implemented. We find that this "one size fits all" assumption is also held by many of our students about a number of teaching methods currently in vogue, such as cooperative learning and whole language instruction. The students imbue the "new" methods with almost magical properties that render them, in and of themselves, capable of improving students' academic standing.

One of our greatest challenges throughout the years has been to help students to understand that a myopic focus on methodology often serves to obfuscate the real issue, which is why in our society, subordinated students do not generally succeed academically in schools? In fact, schools often reproduce the existing asymmetrical power relations among cultural groups.[11] We believe that by taking a sociohistorical view of present-day conditions and concerns that inform the lived experiences of socially perceived minority students, prospective teachers are better able to comprehend the quasi-colonial nature of minority education. By engaging in this critical sociohistorical analysis of subordinated students' academic performance, most of our graduate students (teachers and prospective teachers) are better situated to reinterpret and reframe current educational concerns so as to develop pedagogical structures that speak to the day-to-day reality, struggles, concerns, and dreams of these students. By understanding the historical specificities of marginalized students, these teachers and prospective teachers come to realize that an uncritical focus on methods makes invisible the historical role that schools and their personnel have played (and continue to play), not only in discriminating against many culturally different groups, but also in denying their humanity. By robbing students of their culture, language, history, and values, schools often reduce these students to the status of subhumans who need to be rescued from their "savage" selves. The end result of this cultural eradication and linguicism represents, in our view, a form of dehumanization. Therefore, any discussion having to do with the improvement of subordinated students' academic standing is incomplete if it does not address those discriminatory school practices that lead to dehumanization.

In this chapter we argue that a necessary first step in reevaluating the failure or success of particular instructional methods used with subordinated students calls for a shift in perspective—a shift from a narrow and mechanistic view of instruction to one that is broader in scope and takes into consideration the sociohistorical and political dimensions of education.

We discuss why effective methods are needed for these students, and, why certain strategies are deemed effective or ineffective in a given sociocultural context. Our discussion will include a section that addresses the significance of teachers' understanding of the political nature of education, the reproductive nature of schools, and the schools continued (yet unspoken) deficit views of subordinated students. By conducting a critical analysis of the sociocultural realities in which subordinated students find themselves at school, the implicit and explicit antagonistic relations between students and teachers (and other school representatives) take on focal importance.

As minority instructors who encounter negative race relations that ranged from teachers' outright rejection of subordinated students to their condescending pity, fear, indifference, and apathy when confronted by the challenges of minority student education, we find it surprising that little minority education literature deals explicitly with the very real issue of antagonistic race relations between subordinated students and white school personnel.[12]

For this reason, we also include in this chapter a section that examines the theoretical underpinnings of teaching and learning in two educational approaches. More important, we examine the pedagogical foundations that serve to humanize the educational process, allowing both students and teachers to work toward breaking away from their unspoken antagonism and negative beliefs about each other and get on with the business of sharing and creating knowledge. In the latter part of the chapter, we reanalyze and discuss two instructional methods and approaches identified as effective in current education literature: (1) culturally responsive education; and (2) strategic teaching. We examine these methods for pedagogical underpinnings that— under the critical use of politically clear teachers—have the potential to challenge students academically and intellectually while treating them with dignity and respect. We argue that the informed way in which a teacher implements a method can serve to offset potentially unequal relations and discriminatory structures and practices in the classroom and, in the process, improve the quality of the instructional process for both student and teacher. In other words, politically informed teacher use of methods can create conditions that enable subordinated students to move from their usual passive position to one of active and critical engagement. We are convinced that creating pedagogical spaces that enable students to move *from object to subject position* produces more far-reaching, positive effects than the implementation of a particular teaching methodology, regardless of how technically advanced and promising it may be.

The final section of this article will explore and suggest the implementation of an anti-methods pedagogy that refuses to be enslaved by the rigidity of models and methodological paradigms. An anti-methods pedagogy should be informed by a critical understanding of the sociocultural context that guides our practices so as to free us from the beaten path of methodological certainties and specialisms. *Simply put, it is important that educators not blindly reject teaching methods across the board, but that they reject uncritical appropriation of methods, materials, curricula.* Educators need to reject the present methods fetish so as to create learning environments informed by both action and reflection. In freeing themselves from the blind adoption of so-called effective (and sometimes "teacher-proof") strategies, teachers can begin the reflective process, which allows them to recreate and reinvent teaching methods and materials by always taking into consideration the sociocultural realities that can either limit or expand the possibilities to humanize education. It is important that teachers keep in mind that methods are social constructions that grow out of and reflect ideologies that often prevent teachers from understanding the pedagogical implications of asymmetrical power relations among different cultural groups.

The Significance of Teacher Political Clarity[13]

In his letter to North American educators, Paulo Freire[14] argues that technical expertise and mastery of content area and methodology are insufficient to ensure effective instruction of students from subordinated cultures. Freire contends that, in addition to possessing content area knowledge, teachers must possess political clarity so as to be able to effectively create, adopt, and modify teaching strategies that simultaneously respect and challenge learners from diverse cultural groups in a variety of learning environments.

Teachers working on improving their political clarity recognize that teaching is not a politically neutral undertaking. They understand that educational institutions are socializing institutions that mirror the greater society's culture, values, and norms. Schools reflect both the positive and negative aspects of a society. Thus, the unequal power relations among various social and cultural groups at the societal level are usually reproduced at the school and classroom level, unless concerted efforts are made to prevent their reproduction. Teachers working toward political clarity understand that they can either maintain the status quo or they can work to transform the sociocultural reality at the classroom and school level so that the culture at this micro-level does not reflect macro-level inequalities, such as asymmetrical power relations that relegate certain cultural groups to a subordinate status.

Teachers can support positive social change in the classroom in a variety of ways. One possible intervention can consist of the creation of heterogeneous learning groups for the purpose of modifying low-status roles of individuals or groups of children.[15] In her work, Elizabeth Cohen[16] demonstrates that when teachers create learning conditions where students, especially those perceived as low status (e.g., limited English speakers in a classroom where English is the dominant language, students with academic difficulties, those perceived by their peers for a variety of reasons as less able, etc.), can demonstrate their possession of knowledge and expertise, they are then able to see themselves, and be seen as, capable and competent. As a result, contexts are created in which peers can learn from each other as well.

A teacher's political clarity will not necessarily compensate for structural inequalities that students face outside the classroom; however, teachers can, to the best of their ability, help their students deal with injustices encountered inside and outside the classroom. A number of possibilities exist for preparing students to deal with the greater society's unfairness and inequality that range from engaging in explicit discussions with students about their experiences to more indirect ways (that nevertheless require a teacher who is politically clear), such as creating democratic learning environments where students become accustomed to being treated as competent and able individuals. We believe that the students, once accustomed to the rights and responsibilities of full citizenship in the classroom, will come to expect respectful treatment and authentic estimation in other contexts. Again, it is important to point out that it is not the particular lesson or set of activities that prepares the student; rather, it is the teacher's politically clear educational philosophy that underlies the varied methods and lessons/activities he or she employs that make the difference.

Under ideal conditions, competent educators simultaneously

translate theory into practice *and* consider the population being served and the sociocultural reality in which learning is expected to take place. Let us reiterate that command of a content area or specialization is necessary, but it is not sufficient for effectively working with students. Just as critical is that teachers comprehend that their role as educators is a political act that is never neutral.[17] In ignoring or negating the political nature of their work with these students, teachers not only reproduce the status quo and their students' low status, but they also inevitably legitimize schools' discriminatory practices. For example, teachers who uncritically follow school practices that unintentionally or intentionally serve to promote tracking and segregation within school and classroom contexts continue to reproduce the status quo. Conversely, teachers can become conscious of, and subsequently challenge, the role of educational institutions and their own roles as educators in maintaining a system that often serves to silence students from subordinated groups.

Teachers must also remember that schools, similar to other institutions in society, are influenced by perceptions of socioeconomic status (SES), race/ethnicity, language, or gender.[18] They must begin to question how these perceptions influence classroom dynamics. An important step in increasing teacher political clarity is recognizing that, despite current liberal rhetoric regarding the equal value of all cultures, low-SES and ethnic minority students have historically (and currently) been perceived as deficient. We believe that the present methods-restricted discussion must be broadened to reveal the deeply entrenched deficit orientation toward "difference" (i.e., non-Western European race/ethnicity, non-English-language use, working-class status, femaleness) that prevails in the schools in a deeply "cultural" ideology of white supremacy. As educators, we must constantly be vigilant and ask how the deficit orientation has affected our perceptions concerning students from subordinated populations and created rigid and mechanistic teacher-student relations.[19] Such a model often serves to create classroom conditions in which there is very little opportunity for teachers and students to interact in meaningful ways, establish positive and trusting working relations, and share knowledge.

Our Legacy: A Deficit View of Subordinated Students

As discussed earlier, teaching strategies are neither designed nor implemented in a vacuum. Design, selection, and use of particular teaching approaches and strategies arise from perceptions about learning and learners. We contend that the most pedagogically advanced strategies are sure to be ineffective in the hands of educators who implicitly or explicitly subscribe to a belief system that renders ethnic, racial, and linguistic minority students at best culturally disadvantaged and in need of fixing (if we could only identify the right recipe!), or, at worst, culturally or genetically deficient and beyond fixing.[20] Despite the fact that various models have been proposed to explain the academic failure of certain subordinated groups—academic failure described as *historical, pervasive,* and *disproportionate*—the fact remains that these views of difference are deficit based and deeply imprinted in our individual and collective psyches.[21]

The deficit model has the longest history of any model discussed in the education literature. Richard Valencia[22] traces its evolution over three centuries:

> Also known in the literature as the "social pathology" model or the "cultural deprivation" model, the deficit approach explains disproportionate academic problems among low status students as largely being due to pathologies or deficits in their sociocultural background (e.g., cognitive and linguistic deficiencies, low self-esteem, poor motivation). . . . To improve the educability of such students, programs such as compensatory education and parent-child intervention have been proposed.[23]

Barbara Flores[24] documents the effect this deficit model has had on the schools' past and current perceptions of Latino students. Her historical overview chronicles descriptions used to refer to Latino students over the last century. The terms range from "mentally retarded," "linguistically handicapped," "culturally and linguistically deprived," and "semilingual," to the current euphemism for Latino and other subordinate students: the "at risk" student.

Similarly, research studies continue to lay bare our deficit orientation and its links to discriminatory school practices aimed at students from groups perceived as low status.[25] Findings range from teacher preference for Anglo students to bilingual teachers' preference for lighter-skinned Latino students,[26] to teachers' negative perceptions of working-class parents as compared to middle-class parents,[27] and, finally, to unequal teaching and testing practices in schools serving working-class and ethnic minority students.[28] Especially indicative of our inability to consciously acknowledge the deficit orientation is the fact that the teachers in these studies—teachers from all ethnic groups—were themselves unaware of the active role they played in the differential and unequal treatment of their students.

The deficit view of subordinated students has been critiqued by numerous researchers as ethnocentric and invalid.[29] More recent research offers alternative models that shift the source of school failure away from the characteristics of the individual child, his or her family, and culture, and toward the schooling process.[30] However, we believe that, unfortunately, many of these alternative models often unwittingly give rise to a kinder and more liberal yet more concealed version of the deficit model that views subordinated students as being in need of "specialized" modes of instruction—a type of instructional "coddling" that mainstream students do not require in order to achieve in school. Despite the use of less overtly ethnocentric models to explain the academic standing of subordinated students, we believe that the deficit orientation toward difference, especially as it relates to low socioeconomic and ethnic minority groups, is very deeply ingrained in the ethos of our most prominent institutions, especially schools, and in the various educational programs in place at these sites.

It is against this sociocultural backdrop that teachers can begin to seriously question the unspoken but prevalent deficit orientation used to hide SES, racial/ethnic, linguistic, and gender inequities present in U.S. classrooms. And it is against this sociocultural backdrop that we critically examine two teaching approaches identified by the educational literature as effective with subordinated student populations.

Potentially Humanizing Pedagogy:
Two Promising Teaching Approaches

Well-known approaches and strategies such as cooperative learning, language experience, process writing, reciprocal teaching, and whole language activities can be used to create humanizing learning environments where students cease to be treated as objects and yet receive academically rigorous instruction.[31] However, when these approaches are implemented uncritically, they often produce negative results, as indicated by Lisa Delpit.[32] Critical teacher applications of these approaches and strategies can contribute to discarding deficit views of students from subordinated groups, so that they are treated with respect and viewed as active and capable subjects in their own learning.

Academically rigorous, student-centered teaching strategies can take many forms. One may well ask, is it not merely common sense to promote approaches and strategies that respect, recognize, utilize, and build on students' existing knowledge bases? And the answer would be, of course, yes, it is. However, it is important to recognize, as part of our effort to increase our political clarity, that these practices have *not* typified classroom instruction for students from marginalized populations. The practice of learning from and valuing student language and life experiences *often* occurs in classrooms where students speak a language and possess cultural capital that more closely matches that of the mainstream.[33]

Jean Anyon's[34] classic research suggests that teachers of affluent students are more likely than teachers of working-class students to utilize and incorporate student life experiences and knowledge into the curriculum. For example, in Anyon's study, teachers of affluent students often designed creative and innovative lessons that tapped students' existing knowledge bases; one math lesson, designed to teach students to find averages, asked them to fill out a possession survey inquiring about the number of cars, television sets, refrigerators, and games owned at home so as to teach students to average. Unfortunately, this practice of tapping students' already existing knowledge and language bases is not commonly utilized with student populations traditionally perceived as deficient. Anyon reports that teachers of working-class students viewed them as lacking the necessary cultural capital, and therefore imposed content and behavioral standards with little consideration and respect for student input. Although Anyon did not generalize beyond her sample, other studies suggest the validity of her findings for ethnic minority student populations.[35]

The creation of learning environments for low-SES and ethnic minority students, similar to those for more affluent and white populations, requires that teachers discard deficit notions and genuinely value and utilize students' existing knowledge bases in their teaching. In order to do so, teachers must confront and challenge their own social biases so as to honestly begin to perceive their students as capable learners. Furthermore, they must remain open to the fact that they will also learn from their students. Learning is not only a one-way undertaking, it is also complex and often contradictory, particularly when it takes place under coercive and discriminatory conditions.

Educators need to recognize that no language or set of life experiences is inherently superior, yet our social values reflect our preferences for certain language and life experiences over others. Student-centered teaching strategies such as cooperative learning, language experience, process writing, reciprocal teaching, and whole language activities (if practiced consciously and critically) can help to offset or neutralize our deficit-based failure and recognize subordinated student strengths. Our tendency to discount these strengths occurs whenever we forget that learning only occurs when prior knowledge is accessed and linked to new information.

It is important to understand that learning *is* the act of linking new information to prior knowledge. Accordingly, prior knowledge is stored in memory in the form of knowledge frameworks. New information is understood and stored by calling up the appropriate knowledge framework and then integrating the new information. Acknowledging and using existing student language and knowledge makes good pedagogical sense, and it also constitutes a humanizing experience for students traditionally *de*humanized and disempowered in the schools. We believe that strategies identified as effective in the literature have the potential to offset reductive education in which "the educator as *the one who knows* transfers existing knowledge to the learner as *the one who does not know*."[36] It is important to repeat that mere implementation of a particular strategy or approach (identified as effective) does not guarantee success as the current debate in process writing attests.[37]

Creating learning environments that incorporate student language and life experiences in no way negates teachers' responsibility for providing students with particular academic content knowledge and skills. It is important not to link teacher respect and use of student knowledge and language bases with a laissez-faire attitude toward teaching. It is equally necessary not to confuse academic rigor with rigidity that stifles and silences students. The teacher is the authority, with all the resulting responsibilities that entails; however, it is not necessary for the teacher to become authoritarian in order to challenge students intellectually. Education can be a process in which teacher and students mutually participate in the intellectually exciting undertaking we call learning. Students *can* become active subjects in their own learning, instead of passive objects waiting to be filled with facts and figures by the teacher.

We would like to emphasize that teachers who work with subordinated populations have the responsibility to assist them in appropriating knowledge bases and discourse styles deemed desirable by the greater society. However, this process of appropriation must be additive; that is, the new concepts and new discourse skills must be added to, not subtracted from, the students' existing background knowledge. In order to assume this additive stance, teachers must discard deficit views so they can use and build on life experiences and language styles too often viewed and labeled as "low class" and undesirable. Again, there are numerous teaching strategies and methods that can be employed in this additive manner. For the purposes of illustration, we will briefly discuss two approaches currently identified as promising for students from subordinated populations. The selected approaches are referred to in the literature as culturally responsive instructional approaches and strategic teaching.

Culturally Responsive Instruction:
The Potential to Equalize Power Relations

Culturally responsive instruction grows out of Cultural Difference Theory, which attributes the academic difficulties of students from subordinated groups to cultural incongruence or discontinuities between the learning, language use, and behavioral practices found in the home and those expected by the schools. Ana María Villegas[38] defines culturally responsive instruction as attempts to create instructional situations where teachers use teaching approaches and strategies that recognize and build on culturally different ways of learning, behaving, and using language in the classroom.

A number of classic ethnographic studies document culturally incongruent communication practices in classrooms where students and teachers may speak the same language but use it in different ways. This type of incongruence is cited as a major source of academic difficulties for subordinated students and their teachers.[39] For the purposes of this analysis, one form of culturally responsive instruction, the Kamehameha Education Project reading program, will be discussed.

The Kamehameha Education Project is a reading program developed as a response to the traditionally low academic achievement of native Hawaiian students in Western schools. The reading program was a result of several years of research that examined the language practices of native Hawaiian children in home and school settings. Observations of native Hawaiian children showed them to be bright and capable learners; however, their behavior in the classroom signaled communication difficulties between them and their non-Hawaiian teachers. For example, Kathryn Hu-Pei Au[40] reports that native Hawaiian children's language behavior in the classroom was often misinterpreted by teachers as being unruly and without educational value. She found that the children's preferred language style in the classroom was linked to a practice used by adults in their homes and community called "talk story." She discusses the talk story phenomenon and describes it as a major speech event in the Hawaiian community, where individuals speak almost simultaneously and where little attention is given to turn taking. Au explains that this practice may inhibit students from speaking out as individuals because of their familiarity with and preference for simultaneous group discussion.

Because the non-Hawaiian teachers were unfamiliar with talk story and failed to recognize its value, much class time was spent either silencing the children or prodding unwilling individuals to speak. Needless to say, very little class time was dedicated to other instruction. More important, the children were constrained and not allowed to demonstrate their abilities as speakers and possessors of knowledge. Because the students did not exhibit their skills in mainstream accepted ways (e.g., competing as individuals for the floor), they were prevented from exhibiting knowledge via their culturally preferred style. However, once the children's interaction style was incorporated into classroom lessons, time on task increased, and subsequently, students' performance on standardized reading tests improved. This study's findings conclude that educators can successfully employ the students' culturally valued language practices while introducing the student to more conventional and academically acceptable ways of using language.

It is interesting to note that many of the research studies that examine culturally congruent and incongruent teaching approaches also inadvertently illustrate the equalization of previous asymmetrical power relations between teachers and students. These studies describe classrooms where teachers initially imposed participation structures upon students from subordinated linguistic minority groups and later learned to negotiate with them rules regarding acceptable classroom behavior and language use.[41] Thus these studies, in essence, capture the successful negotiation of power relations that resulted in higher student academic achievement and increased teacher effectiveness. Yet there is little explicit discussion in these studies of the greater sociocultural reality that renders it perfectly normal for teachers to automatically disregard and disrespect subordinated students' preferences and to allow antagonistic relations to foment until they are presented with empirical evidence that legit-imizes the students' practices. Instead, the focus of most of these studies rests entirely on the cultural congruence of the instruction and not on the humanizing effects of a more democratic pedagogy. Villegas[42] accurately critiques the cultural congruence literature when she states:

> It is simplistic to claim that differences in languages used at home and in school are the root of the widespread academic problems of minority children. Admittedly, differences do exist, and they can create communication difficulties in the classroom for both teachers and students. Even so, those differences in language must be viewed in the context of a broader struggle for power within a stratified society.[43]

Despite the focus on the cultural versus the political dimensions of pedagogy, some effort is made to link culturally congruent teaching practices with equalization of classroom power relations. For exam-ple, Au and Mason explain that "one means of achieving cultural con-gruence in lessons may be to *seek a balance between the interactional rights of teachers and students,* so that the children can participate in ways comfortable to them."[44] Their study compared two teachers and showed that the teacher who was willing to negotiate with students either the topic of discussion or the appropriate participation struc-ture was better able to implement her lesson. Conversely, the teacher who attempted to impose both topic of discussion *and* appropriate interactional rules was frequently diverted because of conflicts with students over one or the other.

Unfortunately, as mentioned earlier, interpretations and practical applications of this body of research have focused on the *cultural* con-gruence of the approaches. We emphasize the term "cultural" because in these studies the term "culture" is used in a restricted sense devoid of its dynamic, ideological, and political dimensions. Instead, culture is treated as synonymous with ethnic culture, rather than as "the rep-resentation of lived experiences, material artifacts, and practices *forged within the unequal and dialectical relations* that different groups establish in a given society at a particular point in historical time."[45] We use this definition of culture because, without identifying the political dimensions of culture and subsequent unequal status attributed to members of different ethnic groups, the reader may conclude that teaching methods simply need to be ethnically congruent to be effective—without recognizing that not all ethnic and linguistic cultural groups are viewed and treated as equally legitimate in classrooms. Interestingly enough, there is little discussion of the various socially perceived minority groups' subordinate status vis-à-vis white teachers and peers in these studies. All differences are treated as ethnic cultural differences and not as responses of subordinated students to teachers from dominant groups, and vice versa.

Given the sociocultural realities in the above studies, the specific teaching strategies may not be what made the difference. Indeed, efforts to uncritically export the Kamehameha Education Project reading program to other student populations resulted in failure.[46] It could well be that the teachers' effort to negotiate and share power by treating students as equal participants in their own learning is what made the difference in Hawaii. Just as important is the teachers' willingness to critically interrogate their deficit views of subordinated students. By employing a variety of strategies and techniques, the Kamehameha students were allowed to interact with teachers in egalitarian and meaningful ways. More important, the teachers also learned to recognize, value, use, and build upon students' previously acquired knowledge and skills. In essence, these strategies succeeded in creating a safety zone so students could exhibit their knowledge and skills and, ultimately, empower themselves to succeed in an academic setting. Teachers also benefited from using a variety of student-centered teaching strategies that humanized their perceptions of treatment of students previously perceived as deficient. In his classic study, McDermott [47] reminds us that numerous teaching approaches and strategies can be effective, so long as trusting relations between teacher and students are established and power relations are mutually set and agreed upon.

Strategic Teaching:
The Significance of Teacher-Student Interaction and Negotiation

Strategic teaching refers to an instructional model that explicitly teaches students learning strategies that enable them consciously to monitor their own learning; this is accomplished through the development of reflective cognitive monitoring and metacognitive skills.[48] The goal is to prepare independent and metacognitively aware students. This teaching strategy makes explicit for students the structures of various text types used in academic settings and assists students in identifying various strategies for effectively comprehending the various genres. Although text structures and strategies for dissecting the particular structures are presented by the teacher, a key component of these lessons is the elicitation of students' knowledge about text types and their own strategies for making meaning before presenting them with more conventional academic strategies.

Examples of learning strategies include teaching various text structures (i.e., stories and reports) through frames and graphic organizers. *Frames* are sets of questions that help students understand a given topic. Readers monitor their understanding of a text by asking questions, making predictions, and testing their predictions as they read. Before reading, frames serve as an advance organizer to activate prior knowledge and facilitate understanding. Frames can also be utilized during the reading process by the reader to monitor self-learning. Finally, frames can be used after a reading lesson to summarize and integrate newly acquired information.

Graphic organizers are visual maps that represent text structures and organizational patterns used in texts and in student writing. Ideally, graphic organizers reflect both the content and text structure. Graphic organizers include semantic maps, chains, and concept hierarchies, and assist the student in visualizing the rhetorical structure of the text. Jones and colleagues explain that frames and graphic organizers can be "powerful tools to help the student locate, select, sequence, integrate and restructure information—both from the perspective of understanding and from the perspective of producing information in written responses."[49]

Although much of the research on strategic teaching focuses on English monolingual mainstream students, recent efforts to study linguistic minority students' use of these strategies show similar success. This literature shows that strategic teaching improved the students' reading comprehension as well as their conscious use of effective learning strategies in their native language.[50] Furthermore, these studies show that students, despite limited English proficiency, were able to transfer or apply their knowledge of specific learning strategies and text structure to English reading texts. For example, Hernandez reports that sixth-grade limited-English-proficient students learned, in the native language (Spanish), to generate hypotheses, summarize, and make predictions about readings.[51] According to him: "Students were able to demonstrate use of comprehension strategies even when they could not decode the English text aloud. When asked in Spanish about English texts, the students were able to generate questions, summarize stories, and predict future events in Spanish."[52] Avelar La Salle's study of third- and fourth-grade bilingual students shows that strategic teaching in the native language of three expository text structures commonly found in elementary social studies and science texts (topical net, matrix, and hierarchy) improved comprehension of these types of texts in both Spanish and English.[53]

Such explicit and strategic teaching is most important in the upper elementary grades, where students are expected to focus on the development of more advanced English literacy skills. Beginning at about third grade, students face literacy demands distinct from those encountered in earlier grades. Chall describes the change in literacy demands in terms of stages of readings. She explains that at a stage three of reading, students cease to "learn to read" and begin "reading to learn."[54] Students in third and fourth grade are introduced to content area subjects such as social studies, science, and health. In addition, students are introduced to expository texts (reports). This change in texts, text structures, and in the functions of reading (reading for information) calls for teaching strategies that will prepare students to comprehend various expository texts (e.g., cause/effect, compare/contrast) used across the curriculum.

Strategic teaching holds great promise for preparing linguistic minority students to face the new literacy challenges in the upper grades. As discussed before, the primary goal of strategic instruction is to foster learner independence. This goal in and of itself is laudable. However, the characteristics of strategic instruction that we find most promising grow out of the premise that teachers and students must interact and negotiate meaning as equals in order to reach a goal.

Teachers, by permitting learners to speak from their own vantage points, create learning contexts in which students are able to empower themselves throughout the strategic learning process. Before teachers attempt to instruct students in new content or learning strategies, efforts are made by the teacher to access student prior knowledge so as to link it with new information. In allowing students to present and discuss their prior knowledge and experiences, the teacher legitimizes and treats as valuable student language and cultural experiences usually ignored in classrooms. If students are encouraged to speak on what they know best, then they are, in a sense, treated as experts—experts who are expected to refine their knowledge bases with the additional new content and strategy information presented by the teacher.

Teachers play a significant role in creating learning contexts in which students are able to empower themselves. Teachers act as cultural mentors of sorts when they introduce students not only to the culture of the classroom but to particular subjects and discourse styles as well. In the process, teachers assist the students in appropriating the skills (in an additive fashion) for themselves so as to enable them to behave as "insiders" in the particular subject or discipline. James Gee reminds us that the social nature of teaching and learning must involve apprenticeship into the subject's or discipline's discourse in order for students to do well in school.[55] This apprenticeship includes acquisition of particular content matter, ways of organizing content, and ways of using language (oral and written). Gee adds that these discourses are not mastered solely through teacher-centered and directed instruction but also by "apprenticeship into social practices through scaffolded and supported interaction with people who have already mastered the discourse."[56] The apprenticeship notion can be immensely useful with subordinated students if it facilitates the acceptance and valorization of students' prior knowledge through a mentoring process.

Models of instruction, such as strategic teaching, can promote such an apprenticeship. In the process of apprenticing linguistic minority students, teachers must interact in meaningful ways with them. This human interaction not only assists students in acquiring new knowledge and skills, but it also often familiarizes individuals from different SES and racial/ethnic groups, and creates mutual respect instead of the antagonism that so frequently occurs between teachers and their students from subordinated groups. In this learning environment, teachers and students learn from each other. The strategies serve, then, not to "fix" the student but to equalize power relations and to humanize the teacher-student relationship. Ideally, teachers are forced to challenge implicitly or explicitly held deficit attitudes and beliefs about their students and the cultural groups to which they belong.

Beyond the Politics of Methods

While the two teaching approaches we discussed so far are promising, they will invariably fail in the hands of teachers whose intentions may be good but who lack the necessary political clarity. It is important to understand that, while issues such as teaching strategies and techniques are important, chiefly focusing on technical issues often distracts teachers from the very real ideological and political dimensions of linguistic minority education. We define "political clarity" as the process by which individuals achieve a deepening awareness of the sociopolitical and economic realities that shape their lives and their capacity to transform them. In addition, it refers to the process by which individuals come to better understand possible linkages between macro-level political, economic, and social variables and subordinated groups' academic performance at the micro-level classroom. Thus, it invariably requires that educators struggle to link sociocultural structures and schooling.[57] A related concept, "ideology," refers to the framework of thought that is used by members of a society to justify or rationalize an existing social (dis)order. Thus, "ideological clarity" refers to the process by which individuals struggle to identify both the dominant society's explanations for the existing societal socioeconomic and political hierarchy as well as their own explanation of the social order and any resulting inequalities. Ideological clarity requires that teachers' individual explanations be compared and contrasted with those propagated by the dominant society. The juxtaposing of ideologies, hopefully, forces teachers to better understand if, when, and how their belief systems uncritically reflect those of the dominant society and support unfair and inequitable conditions.

We believe that teacher education programs that enable prospective teachers to, first, recognize the existence of the political dimensions of education and, second, to increase their ideological clarity, will produce the type of intellectual-practitioners we urgently need to teach in the ever-more culturally and socially diverse urban schools of today. It is our belief that uncritical prospective teachers often end up blindly following lockstep methodologies and promulgating unexamined beliefs and attitudes that often compound the difficulties faced by linguistic minority children in school.

Teachers and prospective teachers working on improving their political and ideological clarity recognize that teaching is not a politically or ideologically neutral undertaking. They understand that schools are socializing institutions that often mirror the greater society's culture, values, and norms. Schools reflect both the positive and negative aspects of a society. Thus, the unequal power relations among various social and cultural groups at the societal level are usually reproduced at the school and classroom level, unless, as we have indicated earlier, concerted efforts are made to prevent their reproduction.

It is important to reiterate that while we strongly agree that teachers must be well versed in content area theory and practice, management, and organization, as well as a variety of instructional approaches, it is important to understand that, in addition to these technical skills, we must also be ready to struggle with the greater political and ideological challenges that face us in our attempts to work with subordinated minority populations. In fact, in our opinion, the present assault on bilingual and multicultural education illustrates that these objections to do not necessarily reflect technical or instructional concerns but are, instead, highly political and ideological in nature. That is, opponents of bilingual and multicultural education, in general, do not question specific instructional practices utilized in such programs (such as reading and math instructional techniques, discipline and management approaches, etc.). However, they vociferously oppose linguistic minority students being taught in a language other than English or schools placing too much emphasis on a multicultural curriculum. The opposition is not solely pedagogical in that opponents truly believe that minority students will actually achieve higher if taught in English only. In fact, we argue that their so-called "concern" for linguistic minority academic achievement is not an authentic concern in these debates. Rather, the key concern with using native language instruction grows out of the misperception by the mainstream[58] that using languages other than English (especially Spanish[59]) in school incorrectly accords these languages equal status in relation to English, thus shifting the historically superordinate status of English to one of equality with other, "foreign," languages.[60] In addition, despite the fact that the majority of bilingual teachers are white, middle-class females, mainstream (mis)perceptions are that the bilingual teacher ranks are made up of non-white "ethnics" self-interested in promulgating their various native languages.[61] This (mis)belief also serves to further the mainstream's perceptions that bilingual education threatens to disrupt the existing social order by eventually toppling white English speakers' "rightful" positions of superiority.

Teachers and prospective teachers need to develop the necessary political and ideological clarity to understand what undergirds these attacks. Thus, teacher-educators have the responsibility to provide prospective teachers with—in addition to learning theory and teaching methods—learning opportunities that require that they better understand the political dimensions of education in general, and, in particular, those present in minority education.

The issue of teacher ideology and the role that it may play in teachers' thinking and behavior in education, in general, and in minority education, in particular, has usually been ignored or negated in most teacher education programs as well as in much of the teacher education literature. Historically, we have tended to treat the preparation of teachers as chiefly a technical issue.[62] as Giroux and McLaren so clearly point out that

> As far back as 1890 . . . Horace Willard cogently argued that in contrast to members of other professions, teachers lived "lives of mechanical routine, and were subjected to a machine of supervision, organization, classification, grading, percentages." Forty years later Henry W. Holmes, dean of Harvard University's new Graduate School of Education, echoed these sentiments in his criticism of the National Survey of the Education of Teachers in 1930. According to Holmes, the survey failed to support teachers as independent critical thinkers. Instead, it endorsed a view of the teacher as a "routine worker under the expert direction of principal, supervisors, and superintendents."[63]

Although there have been experimental teacher education programs in the past to develop teachers as critically minded intellectuals or "transformative intellectuals," the dominant tradition has tended to be one that equates teacher preparation with training and imparting of technical skills in instruction, management, and curriculum.[64] The role and effects of teacher political and ideological orientation have not been sufficiently acknowledged as relevant to the task of teacher preparation.

For example, when reviewing last year's 1998 AERA conference program, we were struck by the variety of conference presentations dedicated to discussing teacher "beliefs, " "predispositions," "unconscious perceptions," "assumptions," and their "thoughts" about culturally diverse student populations—culturally diverse, of course, a euphemism for nonwhite and non-middle-class students. [65] Even thought the AERA conference that year made great strides to move beyond views of teacher education as chiefly a technical endeavor, even progressive educators remained somewhat trapped by a euphemistic discourse that fails to interrogate the role of ideology in the creation of inequities and other forms of discrimination along the lines of gender, class, ethnicity, language, and culture.

Educators need to "name" ideology for what it is. Given our history of negating the political nature of education as well as the existence and significance of teacher ideology, it is not surprising to witness that, despite the fact that these are the key issues in current minority education debates today, there is no overt acceptance of this reality by those engaged in the debate. Although there have been, and continue to be, efforts to examine teacher beliefs and attitudes, as illustrated in the AERA conference program example, there have been few systematic attempts to examine the *political and ideological dimensions* of teachers "beliefs," "assumptions," "unconscious perceptions," and how these worldviews are part of a particular ideological orientation. Indeed, teachers' beliefs and attitudes have been treated as apolitical, overly psychologized constructs that "simply" reflect personality types, individual values, and predispositions that have little to do with the existing larger political, social and economic order. Teachers' conscious and unconscious beliefs and attitudes regarding the legitimacy of the greater social order and of the resulting unequal power relations among various cultural groups at the school and classroom levels have, by and large, historically not been acknowledged as significant to improving the educational process and outcome of minority education.

However, even without utilizing the term "ideology," the literature suggests that prospective teachers tend to uncritically and, often, unconsciously hold beliefs and attitudes about the existing social order that reflect the dominant ideology. Unfortunately, this reproduction of thinking often translates into teacher uncritical acceptance of assimilationist and deficit-based views of minority students. We believe that the assimilationist and deficit ideologies held by most white teachers and many nonwhite teachers have had and continue to have detrimental consequences in the education of nonwhite and linguistic minority students.

Assimilationist ideology as used here is treated as synonymous with the concept, "Anglo conformity model," which refers to the belief that immigrants and subordinated indigenous groups should be brought to conform to the practices of the dominant Anglo Saxon culture. Implicit in this belief is that a socioeconomic hierarchy, which results under this system, is an appropriate and fair one that need not be questioned by educators. Rather, educators operating under this ideology argue that the resulting socioeconomic hierarchy is one based on merit; that nonwhite and limited English proficient individuals who want to achieve simply need to learn English and adopt the mainstream culture in order to do so. Yet, we have only to look at African-Americans and Native Americans, rendered English dominant by the forced loss of their native languages, to understand that English-language proficiency in and of itself does not guarantee first-class citizenship.

The combination of assimilationist belief system with a deficit ideology proves to be an especially deadly one because it rationalizes disrespecting linguistic minority students' native language and primary culture, misteaching them dominant culture and English, and then blaming their academic difficulties on the students' "pathological deficiencies."

The elements of both harmful assimilationist and deficit ideologies are powerfully captured in the research of Elizabeth Howard.[66] In her research, Howard set out to describe teachers' beliefs regarding how to best educate limited English proficient students. Although her intended focus was to examine both sets of teachers' beliefs about actual instructional practices and theories, she inadvertently also describes a school situation where the white monolingual teachers are engaged in an "ideological war" against their bilingual counterparts.

Howard describes a situation where some monolingual English-speaking teachers resort to disrespectful attacks against Latina teachers when voicing their opposition to using Spanish for instructional purposes (bilingual education). The English monolingual teachers do not present their opposition in terms of pedagogical theory but, instead, attack the Latina teachers' English-language ability and describe it as faulty. Furthermore, they criticize the Latina teachers' Spanish-language proficiency despite the fact that they do not speak the language! While English monolingual teachers are eager to question bilingual teachers' proficiency in English, they remain silent about the lack of proficiency of most foreign language teachers in the target language they teach. In fact, even though foreign language education has been a general failure, it has sustained very little criticism as compared to attacks on bilingual education.

As illustrated in our discussion, too often prospective teachers come into teacher education programs having unconsciously absorbed assimilationist and deficit views of nonwhites and the poor. This ideological stance often constitutes the foundation on which future teacher training will be built. The reality is that most prospective teachers have not been forced to critically reflect on their ideological orientation and "bring with them, unintentional or otherwise, racist and xenophobic views with the potential to corrupt teacher-student interactions and academic instruction."[67] The restricted perspectives from which some teachers view their students is a product of their own personal folk theories, internalized beliefs, and values that reflect their own formative and restricted life and cultural experiences and influences. However, they do not recognize their beliefs and attitudes as reflecting the dominant ideology but instead view them as "natural," "objective," and "commonsense"—in other words: *the norm*.[68] Despite the reality that one's ideology serves as a lens that filters new information or knowledge, conventional teacher education programs (bilingual and English monolingual) fail to acknowledge its existence and treat preservice teachers as blank slates who simply need to learn the latest in teaching and discipline techniques to function effectively in the linguistic minority classroom.

The dramatic increase in poor, nonwhite, and limited-English-proficient students in U.S. public schools also signals the urgent need to understand and challenge the ideological orientations of prospective teachers in teacher education programs. One current challenge is to adequately prepare the overwhelmingly white, female, and middle-class preservice teacher population to work with subordinated student groups, which are quickly becoming the majority in many of the largest urban public schools in the country.[69] While the nation's school population is made up of approximately 40 percent minority children, nearly 90 percent of teachers are white.[70] In addition, social class differences between teacher and student continue to widen. For example 44 percent of African-American children and 36 percent of Latino children live in poverty, yet more teachers come from white lower-middle- and middle-class homes and have been reared in rural and suburban communities.[71]

Furthermore, there are also significant differences in teacher-student language backgrounds. The majority of teachers are English monolingual while estimates of school-age limited English proficient students in the public schools range from 5 to 7.5 million.[72] Even in bilingual education, the majority of teachers are white, which points to the common misperception that nonwhite teachers fill the majority of bilingual teacher slots. The reality is that only 10 percent of teacher positions are held by Latinos.[73] In addition, while Hispanic students constitute two-thirds of limited-English-proficient students, only 15 percent of bilingual teachers are Hispanic.[74]

Given these changing student demographics, it becomes evident that *all* teachers, not just bilingual teachers, are responsible for preparing linguistic minority and limited-English-proficient children. And, given the social class, cultural, and language differences between teachers and students, it becomes especially urgent that teachers critically understand their ideological orientations with respect to cultural and class differences so they can begin to comprehend that teaching is not a politically or ideologically neutral undertaking.

Although the need to help teacher and prospective teachers "name" and interrogate their ideological stance is urgent, it is not an easy task. The reality that educators unknowingly accept and support the status quo even when it can potentially harm their students is unfortunate but it is not surprising. As Pierre Bourdieu so succinctly states,

> Teachers are the products of a system whose aim is to transmit an aristocratic culture, and are likely to adopt its values with greater ardor in proportion to the degree to which they owe it their own academic and social success. How indeed could they

avoid unconsciously bringing into play the values of the milieu from which they come, or to which they wish to belong, when teaching and assessing their pupils? Thus, in higher education, the working or lower middle class student will be judged according to the scale of values of the educated classes which many teachers owe to their social origin and which they willingly adopt. . . .[75]

Current research on prospective teachers' beliefs, attitudes, and preferences suggests that they prefer to teach students who are like themselves in communities that are familiar to them. Most preservice teachers very clearly state that they do not want to teaching in inner-city schools or work with minority or limited-English-proficient students.[76]

Approaches for preparing prospective teachers to deal with increasing cultural and linguistic diversity in schools can, with few exceptions, be described as fragmented additions to the existing teacher preparation curriculum. While most teacher education programs have begun to acknowledge issues of cultural and linguistic diversity (not difference), they usually do so by requiring only one or two courses in multicultural education or electives that discuss cultural, ethnic, or gender issues.[77] Few programs have seriously attempted to infuse or permeate the existing teacher education curriculum with key concepts that require prospective teachers to critically examine and interrogate their ideological orientations as part of their learning process.[78] Critics of fragmented multicultural education claim that it fails to seriously address issues of structural and ideological inequality or to challenge prospective teachers' ethnocentric and culturally parochial ideologies. Because of these limited and superficial attempts to prepare teachers for meeting the needs of children from subordinated groups, there is little opportunity for them to begin to develop political and ideological clarity.

In fact, the majority of studies that examine changes in prospective teacher beliefs and attitudes after experiencing multicultural education report that they do not significantly change their racist and classist views of minority and poor students. Instead, the instruction often serves to make the students more strongly embrace their existing ethnocentric attitudes and beliefs regarding poor and nonwhite populations.[79]

In addition to failing to produce significant changes in teachers' ideologies, a growing body of research effectively documents how prospective teachers resist information and knowledge that conflicts with their ideological orientations. For example, prospective teachers often report feeling guilt, anger, shame, and despair when dealing with subjects concerning racism and inequalities within the existing social order.[80] These prospective teachers' emotional responses often impair their intellectual understanding and mastery of the material being presented. In fact, a few studies capture the antagonistic manner in which preservice teachers respond to their multicultural education instructors.[81]

One could argue that it appears nearly impossible to improve the preparation of teachers since the education faculty usually resembles the prospective teachers in ethnic and class makeup and lack precisely the type of cross-class and cross-cultural experiences that they expect the prospective teachers to acquire.[82] The majority of teacher educators are male and white and most probably do not possess the expertise necessary to address the preparation of teachers for diversity.[83] In addition, the argument has been made that the majority of preservice teachers may not be developmentally capable of engaging in the type of critical analysis necessary to achieve greater ideological and political clarity and that it is futile to attempt to produce the types of changes in teacher ideology needed for effective teaching of poor and nonwhite students.[84]

We would argue, however, that the restricted perspectives by which some teachers view their minority students is not fixed and irreversible. Teachers' actions and beliefs that eventually contradict the dominant norms serve as evidence that the individual is a creator as well as a recipient of values, and many members of the dominant culture, as well as subordinated cultures, are open to recognizing the political dimensions of teaching, questioning the status quo, and working toward creating more just and democratic educational conditions for all students.[85] In our view, instead of falling prey to a form of cynicism that infantilizes teachers, we would propose a radical transformation in teacher preparation where political and ideological clarity are prioritized.

In fact, we believe that much can be learned from effective teachers of minority students and applied to our thinking about the types of concepts and learning experiences prospective teachers should encounter in teacher preparation programs. Current efforts to identify the characteristics of exemplary teachers suggest that successful teachers share an anti-assimilationist and anti-deficit ideological orientation. That is, the teachers in these studies question, in one form or another, the "correctness" or "fairness" of the existing social order and actively work to prevent its reproduction at the school and classroom levels. Ideas for improving the preparation of teachers can be drawn from these exemplary teachers' ideological orientations and resulting practices.

What is needed in many teacher preparation programs is commitment, on the part of administrators and educators, to weave key concepts such as political and ideological clarity, courage, solidarity, and ethics across the existing curriculum in order to better prepare prospective teachers to become effective teachers of all students, but in particular, of subordinated minority students.

Prospective teachers and existing teachers must develop ideological and political clarity that will guide them in their denouncement of a discriminatory school and social context so as to protect and advocate for their students. In addition, this clarity will also serve to help them move beyond the present so as to announce a future that imagines a utopia where social justice and a humanizing pedagogy are always present in our classrooms.

According to Paulo Freire, beyond technical skills, teachers should also be equipped with a full understanding of what it means to have courage—to denounce the present inequities that directly cripple certain populations of students—and effectively create psychologically harmless educational contexts.[86] He challenges us to become courageous in our commitment to defend subordinated student populations even when it is easier not to take a stand.

In addition to ideological and political clarity and courage, prospective teachers must see themselves in solidarity with their students and their students' communities. They must understand the meaning and risk of solidarity so as to protect the dignity of their students. Again, actions of solidarity require politically and ideologically clear, courageous individuals, as demonstrated by many of the effective teachers discussed in the previous section.

Schools of education should also create spaces where the development of an ethical posture informs, not only the technical acquisition of skills, but also one's position vis-à-vis the human suffering that certain populations of students face in their community and in their school. All too often, in our quest to become "culturally relativistic" we fail to discuss the ethical and moral dimensions of our work as educators. Regardless of the diversity of "cultural" opinions found in any school of education, concepts such as "equality," "democracy," "fairness," "justice" need to serve as ever-present anchors across the teacher education curriculum so as to remind prospective teachers that teaching is ultimately a moral and ethical undertaking. Such an undertaking requires a high level of commitment and political clarity so as to enable educators to learn what happens in the world of their students, their dreams and their struggles. In addition to the mastery of the content of one's field of specialization, political and ideological clarity becomes a decisive factor in effective teaching and learning. As one cannot be a successful teacher without a rigorous content preparation, one cannot be effective pedagogically without the political and ideological clarity that would force one to ask the a priori political question: What content, against what, for whom, and against whom? Thus, the role of a teacher can never be reduced to a facile and mechanistic transmission of selective content. The role of a teacher is invariably political, as eloquently argued by Paulo Freire:

> My very presence in the school as a teacher is intrinsically a
> political presence, something that students cannot possibly
> ignore. In this sense, I ought to transmit to the students my
> capacity to analyze, to compare, to evaluate, to decide, to opt, to
> break with. My capacity to be just, to practice justice, and to
> have a political presence. And as a presence, I cannot sin by

omission. I am, by definition, a subject "destined" to choose. To have options. I honor truth. And all that means being ethical. . . . If I have made a choice for open-minded democratic practice, then obviously this excludes reactionary, authoritarian, elitist attitudes and actions. Under no circumstances, therefore, may I discriminate against a student.[87]

The Pedagogy of Political Clarity

Unfortunately, the debate over political clarity is often structured in a false and reductionistic binarism where the emphasis on political clarity invariably de-emphasizes the mastery of the content of one's field of socialization. In other words, it is often assumed that once teachers begin to develop political clarity, automatically the content suffers. The converse argument is also frequent, where the effective teaching of content must preclude any political linkage. What is important to note is that the latter position constitutes, in itself, a political act, rendering political neutrality an impossibility. Hence, politics is inextricable from content and vice versa. What is pedagogically unsound is the capricious dismissal of one over the other. The following example illustrates our position. Pepi Leistyna, a graduate of the Harvard Graduate School of Education, recounts his experiences in an exercise designed to teach students the value of multiple perspectives:

> The course was centered around having the whole class observe the moon for the entire semester. As such, each and every day was dedicated to a discussion of what different people saw in the night skies. Another typical classroom exercise consisted of attaching a string to our nose, with the opposite end fixed to a mirror on the ceiling, so we could see each other from various angles. There were also show-and-tell sessions in which some students presented their own personal crayon drawings to the entire class. This was all done in the name of "understanding individual differences and alternative perspectives."
>
> As these inane exercises continued week after week, I could not understand how this type of pedagogy would help develop

self-reflective, multilensed, and critical researchers and practitioners. In addition, I could not help but wonder what any of this had to do with the fact that schools and streets are virtual war zones where drug abuse, teenage pregnancy, school dropouts, illiteracy, and a long list of oppressive practices and social injustices that directly affect the educational process are running rampant. How would the methodology of this particular graduate course help teachers to understand the dialectical relationship between intergroup strife and struggle and individual psychology?

At one point during the semester, the class participated in observing two young black girls engage in a cognitive exercise of solving puzzles. In light of the current debates and conflicts concerning poverty, racism, sexism, and other forms of discrimination, especially the media blitz around the release of Richard Hernstein and Charles Murray's *The Bell Curve* (1994), a book that makes claims to the genetic inferiority of blacks and other groups, I was extremely uncomfortable with a room full of privileged white people (only one black male) handing over two black girls for the sake of clinical observation. This was especially difficult for me in the sense that we as a group did not problematize the realities that have led these two individuals (members of a collective that continues to experience a great deal of oppression in this country) to attend by choice an African-American private school. The fact that in order to maintain their own cultural capital and avoid total domination they self-segregated themselves to an environment that nurtures and respects them was ignored by the roomful of budding researchers.

Finding this radical omission disconcerting, to say the least, I openly expressed to the class the importance of context in understanding the multiple and contingent social identities of people, and how such social identities within unequal relations of power invoke particular kinds of behavior and interaction. When I asked why, as a group, we had neglected to make the connections between the current national debates of what Harvard represents as an "elite," predominantly white institution, the sociopolitical realities of these young, low socioeconomic-status black girls, and the contingent nature of cognition, the professor responded, "This is one important and complex set of questions to look at. I think that one can also look at other things."[88]

While this Harvard professor summarily dismissed Leystina's suggestion to link the lesson on the worth of accepting multiple perspectives with the sociocultural reality of the two African-American girls being observed by the class, a high school teacher, Bill Bigelow, had no difficulties utilizing a sphere object like the moon to create pedagogical spaces in his Global Studies classroom so as to enable students to read the multiple realities linked with a soccer ball. According to Bill Bigelow, he began the lesson with a beat-up soccer ball that "sat in a plastic container on a stool in the middle of the circle of student desks."[89] He asked students to write a description of the soccer ball as he urged them to "feel free to get up and look at it. There is no right or wrong. Just describe the ball however you'd like."[90]

As expected, he was greeted with "puzzlement and annoyance," since, according to one student, "it's just a soccer ball." The teacher wanted students to write "just a paragraph or two" in reference to the soccer ball. As he had anticipated, the students' "accounts were straightforward and accurate if uninspired" as captured in the following description of the ball:

> The ball is a sphere which has white hexagons and black pentagons. The black pentagons contained red stars, sloppily outlined in silver. . . .One of the hexagons contains a green rabbit wearing a soccer uniform with "Euro 88" written parallel to the rabbit's body. Another hexagon has the number of patches that the ball contains.[91]

Although the students provided an accurate descriptive account of the ball, their writing remained purely at the level of descriptions, with little connection to a "deeper social reality associated with this ball—a reality that advertising and consumption-oriented rhythms of U.S. daily life discouraged students from considering the label, "Made in Pakistan." We would argue that the students were not only discouraged to read the world that gave life to the soccer ball by the "advertising and consumption-oriented rhythms of U.S. daily life," but schools, by and large produce a disarticulation of an object of knowledge by dislodging it from a critical and coherent comprehension of the world that informs and sustains it. This disarticulation of knowledge anesthetizes consciousness, without which one can never develop clarity of reality, limiting students, at best, to a mere descriptive level of reading and, at worse, rendering them stupidified and unable to make linkages between the reading of the word and the world.

We are not at all surprised that the Harvard professor would dismiss a proposal that would link the object of knowledge with the sociocultural reality of the two African-American students. Most educators, particularly conservative educators, view such linkage as politicizing education. What those educators fail to acknowledge is that only a politicized person is able to sort out the different and often fragmented bodies of knowledge contained in the reading of the word so as to be able to read the world. These educators also conveniently ignore that the apprehension of clarity requires a high level of political awareness that can be achieved through the influx of information and relating of each piece to another so as to gain a global comprehension of the facts and their raison d'être.

It is the articulation of multiple bodies of knowledge so as to gain a more critical understanding of reality that motivated Bill Bigelow to invite his students to inquire about "the human lives hidden in 'just a soccer a ball'—a clue to the invisible Pakistanis whose hands crafted the ball sitting in the middle of the classroom." Aware of the importance of making linkages, Bigelow cleverly used Bertolt Brecht's poem "A Worker Reads History" as a pedagogical strategy to engage his students in a deeper meaning contained in the hidden stories of the soccer ball:

Who built the seven gates of Thebes?
The books are filled with names of kings.

Was it kings who hauled the craggy blocks of stone?
In the evening when the Chinese wall was finished
Where did the masons go? Imperial Rome
Is full of arcs of triumph. Who reared them up?
Young Alexander conquered India.
He alone?
Caesar beat the Gauls.
Was there not even a cook in his army?
Each page a victory.
At whose expense, the victory bull?
Every ten years a great man,
Who paid the piper?[92]

Bill Bigelow's use of Bertolt Brecht's poem was not only a brilliant pedagogical strategy, but it also eclipsed the run-of-the mill criticism that alleges that the development of political clarity invariably leads to the politicization of education, which, in turn, waters down the curriculum. Who would argue that reading Bertolt Brecht is watering down education? On the other hand, Brecht's poem served as a tool that enabled the teacher to invite his students to engage in rigorous inquiry as a process to unveil the hidden realities contained in he soccer ball made in Pakistan. After reading the poem, the teacher asked his students to "re-see this soccer ball. If you like, you can write from the point of view of the ball, you can ask the ball questions, but I want you to look at it deeply. What did we miss the first time around? It's not 'just a soccer ball.'" According to the teacher, "[v]ersions one and two were night and day" when students began to make linkages that enabled them read beyond the descriptive level. Questions such as "Who built this soccer ball?" and "Where did the real people go after it was made?" began to be raised. These critical questions began to slowly unveil what have been hidden, which led a student named Sarah to write the following:

I sew together these shapes of leather. I stab my finger with my needle. I feel a small pain, but nothing much, because my fingers are so callused. Everyday I sew these soccer balls together for 5 cents, but I've never once had a chance to play soccer with may friends. I sew and sew all day long to have these balls shipped to another place where they represent fun. Here, they represent the hard work of everyday life.[93]

When we compare the first description of the soccer ball with Sarah's more in-depth reading of the world contained in the soccer ball, it becomes clear how political clarity not only expands the range of possibilities for meaning making but also renders the quality of writing immensely more substantive and eloquent. As the teacher, Bill Bigelow, clearly puts it, "[S]tudents had begun to image the humanity inside the ball: their pieces were vivid and curious. The importance of making visible the invisible, of looking behind masks presented by everyday consumer goods, became a central theme in my first-time effort to teach about the 'global sweatshops' and child labor in poor countries."[94] The important lesson we learned from Bill Bigelow is that Global Studies as a course of study should not be restricted to the romantization of the great deeds as powerfully suggested by Brecht's poem. That is, we need also to look at Global Studies through a magnifying glass so we can begin to see the grotesque and barbaric images hidden in the victory arcs or Michael Jordan's seductive Nike commercials so as to denude the human exploitation of children making soccer balls so developed-country children can have fun cheaply on the hide of children in the third world who have been destined to a life of human misery and exploitation.

Bill Bigelow's pedagogy shows that the development of political awareness should not be restricted to a particular course curriculum. It should be woven throughout the general curriculum so as to open possibilities to think otherwise. What becomes clear is that the more political aware one becomes, the greater the opportunity to achieve conscientization. Thus, political clarity, as Paulo Freire, suggested, is the only means through which "the less coherent sensibility of the world begins to be surpassed and more rigorous intellectual pursuits give rise to a more coherent comprehension of the world."[95] Thus, in order to go beyond a mere world-level reading of the moon (in the case of the Harvard graduate course) and the soccer ball (in the case of

Bill Bigelow's class), we must develop a critical comprehension of the cultural, social, economic, and political practices that constitute the world before can make sense of the word-level description of the spherical reality of both the moon and the soccer ball.

Beyond Teaching Strategies: Towards a Humanizing Pedagogy

When we recall a special education teacher's experience related in a bilingualism and literacy course that author Bartolomé taught, we are reminded of the humanizing effects of teaching strategies that allow teachers to listen, learn from, and mentor their students. This teacher, for most of her career, had been required to assess her students through a variety of close-ended instruments and then to remediate their diagnosed "weaknesses" with discrete skills instruction. The assessment instruments provided little information to explain why students either answered a question correctly or incorrectly, and they often confirmed perceived student academic, linguistic, and cognitive weaknesses. This fragmented discrete skills approach to instruction restricts the teacher's access to existing student knowledge and experiences not specifically elicited by the academic tasks. Needless to say, this teacher knew very little about her students other than her deficit descriptions of them.

As part of the requirements in Bartolomé's course, she was asked to focus on one Spanish-proficient, limited-English-proficient special education student over the semester. She observed the student in a number of formal and informal contexts, and she engaged him in a number of open-ended tasks. These tasks included allowing him to write entire texts such as stories and poems (despite diagnosed limited English proficiency) and to engage in think-alouds[96] during reading. Through these open-ended activities, the teacher learned about her student's English writing ability (both strengths and weaknesses), his life experiences and worldviews, and his meaning-making strategies for reading. Consequently, the teacher not only constructed an instructional plan much better suited to her student's academic needs and interests; even more important, *she* underwent a humanizing process that allowed her to recognize the varied and valuable life experiences and knowledge her student brought into the classroom.

This teacher was admirably candid when she shared her initial negative and stereotypic views of the student and her radical transformation. Despite this teacher's mastery of content area, her lack of political clarity blinded her to the oppressive and dehumanizing nature of instruction offered to linguistic minority students. Initially, she had formed an erroneous notion of her student's personality, worldview, academic ability, motivation, and academic potential on the basis on his Puerto Rican ethnicity, low-SES background, limited English proficiency, and moderately learning-disabled label. Because of the restricted and closed nature of earlier assessment and instruction, the teacher had never received information about her student that challenged her negative perceptions. Listening to her student and in reading his poetry and stories, she discovered his loving and sunny personality, learned his personal history, and identified academic strengths and weaknesses. In the process, she discovered and challenged her deficit orientation. The following excerpt exemplifies the power of the student voice for humanizing teachers.

My Father

I love my father very much. I will never forget what my father has done for me and my brothers and sisters. When we first came from Puerto Rico we didn't have food to eat and we were very poor. My father had to work three jobs to put food and milk on the table. Those were hard times and my father worked so hard that we hardly saw him. But even when I didn't see him, I always knew he loved me very much. I will always be grateful to my father. We are not so poor now and so he works only one job. But I will never forget what my father did for me. I will also work to help my father have a better life when I grow up. I love my father very much.

The process of learning about her student's rich and multifaceted background enabled this teacher to move beyond the rigid methodology that had required her to distance herself from the student and to confirm the deficit model to which she unconsciously adhered to. In this case, the meaningful teacher-student interaction served to equalize the teacher-student power relations and to humanize instruction by expanding the horizons through which the student demonstrated human qualities, dreams, desires, and capacities that close-ended tests and instruction never captured.

We believe that the specific teaching methods utilized by the teacher, in and of themselves, were not the significant factors. The actual strengths of methods depend, first and foremost, on the degree to which they embrace a humanizing pedagogy that values the students' background knowledge, culture, and life experiences and creates learning contexts where power is shared by students and teachers. Teaching methods are means to an end; that is, humanizing education to promote academic success for students historically under-serviced by the schools. A teaching strategy is a vehicle to a greater goal. A number of vehicles exist that may or may not lead to a humanizing pedagogy depending on the sociocultural reality in which teachers and students operate. Teachers need to examine critically these promising teaching strategies and appropriate the aspects of those strategies that work best in their particular learning environments. Too often, teachers uncritically adopt "the latest in methodology" and blame the students (once again) when the method proves ineffective.

We believe that educators would be far more effective if they critically understood the complex interrelationship of sociocultural factors shaping the educational context within which they are expected to teach subordinate students. The teachers' high level of critical awareness would enable them to develop the necessary pedagogical structures that cease to view and treat students from subordinate populations as lacking or deficient. Finally, we would urge educators to understand that, above all, the critical issue is the degree to which we hold the moral conviction that we must humanize the educational experience of students from subordinate populations by eliminating the hostility that often confronts these students. This process would require that we cease to be overly dependent on methods as technical instruments and adopt a pedagogy that seeks to forge a cultural democracy where all students are treated with respect and dignity. A true cultural democracy forces teachers to recognize that students' lack of familiarity with the dominant values of the curriculum "does not mean . . . that the lack of these experiences develop in these children a different 'nature' that determines their absolute incompetence."[97]

Unless educational methods are situated into the students' cultural experiences, students will continue to show difficulty in mastering content area that is not only alien to their reality but is often antagonistic toward their culture and lived experiences. Otherwise, not only will these methods continue to fail students, particularly those from subordinate groups, but they will never lead to the creation of schools as true cultural democratic sites. For this reason, it is imperative that teachers problematize the prevalent notion of "magical" methods and incorporate an anti-methods pedagogy, a process through which teachers (1) critically deconstruct the ideology that informs the methods fetish prevalent in education, (2) understand the intimate relationships between methods and the theoretical underpinnings that inform these methods, and (3) evaluate the pedagogical consequences of blindly and uncritically replicating methods without regard to the subordinate status along the lines of cultural, class, gender and linguistic difference. In short, we need an anti-methods pedagogy that adheres to Freire's insightful comments concerning the role of the educator:

> It becomes obvious that she/he will never develop a truly "critical" perspective as a teacher by indulging in mechanical memorization on the rhythmic repetition of phrases and ideas at the expense of creative challenge. Intellectuals who memorize everything, reading for hours on end, slaves to the text, fearful of taking risks, speaking as if they were reciting from memory, fail to make any concrete connections between what they have read and what is taking place in the world, the country, or the local community. They repeat what has been read with precision but rarely teach anything of personal value. They speak cor-

rectly about dialectical thought but think mechanistically. Such teachers inhabit an idealized world, a world of mere data, disconnected from the one most people inhabit.[98]

NOTES

1. P. Freire, *Pedagogy of Freedom: Ethics, Democracy, and Civic Courage* (Boulder, CO: Rowman & Littlefield Publishers, 1998), p. xxxx.

2. The term "technical" refers to the positivist tradition in education that presents teaching as a precise and scientific undertaking and teachers as technicians responsible for carrying out (preselected) instructional programs and strategies.

3. "Subordinated" refers to cultural groups that are politically, socially, and economically subordinate in the greater society. While individual members of these groups may not consider themselves subordinate in any manner to the white "mainstream," they nevertheless are members of a greater collective that historically has been perceived and treated as subordinate and inferior by the dominant society. Thus it is not entirely accurate to describe these students as "minority" students, since the term connotes numerical minority rather than the general low status (economic, political, and social) these groups have held, and that I think is important to recognize when discussing their historical academic underachievement.

4. American Association of School Administrators, *Raising Achievement Among Minority Students* (Arlington, VA, 1987). T. P. Carter and M. L. Chatfield, "Effective Bilingual Schools: Implications for Policy and Practice," *American Journal of Education* 95 (1986), pp. 200-232. T. Lucas, R. Henze and R. Donato, 1990, "Promoting the Success of Latino Language-Minority Students: An Exploratory Study of Six High Schools," *Harvard Educational Review* 60 (1990), pp. 315-340. W. Tikunoff, *Applying Significant Bilingual Instructional Features in the Classroom* (Rosslyn, VA: National Clearinghouse for Bilingual Education, 1985).

5. B. McLeod (ed.), *Cultural Diversity and Second Language Learning* (Albany: State University of New York, 1994). M. S. Knapp and P. M. Shields, *Better Schooling for the Children of Poverty: Alternatives to Conventional Wisdom*, vol. 2, Commissioned Papers and Literature Reviews (Washington, D.C.: U.S. Department of Education, 1990). J. V. Tinajero and A. F. Ada, *The Power of Two Languages: Literacy and Biliteracy for Spanish-Speaking Students* (New York: MacMillan/McGraw-Hill, 1993).

6. M. Reyes, "Challenging Venerable Assumptions: Literacy Instruction for Linguistically Different Students," *Harvard Educational Review* 62 (1991), pp. 427-446.

7. Ibid., p. 435.

8. For an example of this research, see L. A. Vogt, C. Jordan, and R. G. Tharp, "Explaining School Failure, Producing School Success: Two Cases," *Anthropology & Education Quarterly* 18 (1987), pp. 276-286.

9. L. Delpit, "The Silenced Dialogue: Power and Pedagogy in Educating Other People's Children," in *Other People's Children: Cultural Conflict in the Classroom* (New York: The New Press, 1995).

10. Ibid., pp. 31-32.

11. J. Anyon, "Social Class and the Hidden Curriculum of Work," in J. R. Gress (ed.), *Curriculum: An Introduction to the Field* (Berkeley, CA: McCutchan, 1988), pp. 366-389. M. Gibson and J. Ogbu, *Minority Status and Schooling: A Comparative Study of Immigrant and Involuntary Minorities* (New York, Garland, 1991). H. Giroux, *Border Crossing: Cultural Workers and the Politics of Education* (New York: Routledge, 1992). P. Freire, *The Politics of Education: Culture, Power and Liberation* (South Hadley, MA: Bergin & Garvey, 1985).

12. For more in-depth discussion of this phenomenon, see J. Ogbu, "Variability in Minority Responses to Schooling: Nonimmigrants vs. Immigrants," in G. Spindler and L. Spindler (eds.), *Interpretive Ethnography of Education* (Hillsdale, NJ: Lawrence Erlbaum Associates, 1987), pp. 255-280. H. Giroux, *Border Crossing: Cultural Workers and the Politics of Education.*

13. Political clarity refers to the process by which individuals achieve a deepening awareness of the sociopolitical and economic realities that shape their lives and their capacity to recreate them. In addition, it refers to the process by which individuals come to better understand possible linkages between macro-level political, economic, and social variables and subordinate group academic performance at the micro-level classroom. Thus, it invariably requires linkages between sociocultural structures and schooling.

14. P. Freire, "Letter to North American Educators," in I. Shor (ed.), *Freire for the Classroom* (Portsmouth, NJ: Boynton/Cook, 1987), pp. 211-214.

15. Elizabeth Cohen explains that in the society at large there are status distinctions made on the basis of social class, ethnic group, and gender. These status distinctions are often reproduced at the classroom level, unless teachers make conscious efforts to prevent this reproduction.

16. E. G. Cohen, *Designing Groupwork: Strategies for the Heterogeneous Classroom* 2d ed., (New York: Teachers College Press, 1994).

17. P. Freire, *The Politics of Education: Culture, Power and Liberation.* P. Freire, "Letter to North American Educators." P. Freire and D. Macedo, *Literacy: Reading the Word and the World* (South Hadley, MA: Bergin & Garvey, 1987).

18. J. Anyon, "Social Class and the Hidden Curriculum of Work." G. M. Bloom, "The Effects of Speech Style and Skin Color on Bilingual Teaching Candidates' and Bilingual Teachers' Attitudes Toward Mexican American Pupils," unpublished doctoral dissertation, Stanford University, 1991. J. Cummins, *Empowering Minority Students* (Sacramento: California Association of Bilingual

Education, 1989). J. Ogbu, "Variability in Minority Responses to Schooling: Nonimmigrants vs. Immigrants."

19. J. Cummins, *Empowering Minority Students*. H. Giroux and P. McLaren, "Teacher Education and the Politics of Engagement: The Case for Democratic Schooling," *Harvard Educational Review* 56 (1986), pp. 213-238. B. Flores, P. T. Cousin, and E. Diaz, "Critiquing and Transforming the Deficit Myths About Learning, Language and Culture," *Language Arts* 68 no. 5 (1991), pp. 369-379.

20. For detailed discussions regarding various deficit views of subordinate students over time, see B. Flores, P.T. Cousin, and E. Diaz, "Critiquing and Transforming the Deficit Myths About Learning, Language and Culture."

21. B. M. Flores, "Language Interference of Influence: Toward a Theory for Hispanic Bilingualism," unpublished doctoral dissertation, University of Arizona at Tucson, 1982. "Interrogating the Genesis of the Deficit View of Latino Children in the Educational Literature During the 20th Century," paper presented at the American Educational Research Association Conference Atlanta (April 1993). M. Menchaca and R. Valencia "Anglo-Saxon Ideologies in the 1920s-1930s: Their Impact on the Segregation of Mexican Students in California," *Anthropology & Education Quarterly* 21 (1990), pp. 222-245. R. Valencia "Minority Academic Underachievement: Conceptual and Theoretical Considerations for Understanding the Achievement Problems of Chicano Students," paper presented to the Chicano Faculty Seminar, Stanford University (November 25, 1986); *Chicano School Failure and Success: Research and Policy Agendas for the 1990s* (New York: Falmer Press, 1991).

22. R. Valencia "Minority Academic Underachievement: Conceptual and Theoretical Considerations for Understanding the Achievement Problems of Chicano Students."

23. Ibid., p. 3.

24. B. M. Flores, "Language Interference of Influence: Toward a Theory for Hispanic Bilingualism"; "Interrogating the Genesis of the Deficit View of Latino Children in the Educational Literature During the 20th Century."

25. J. Anyon, "Social Class and The Hidden Curriculum of Work." G. M. Bloom, "The Effects of Speech Style and Skin Color on Bilingual Teaching Candidates' and Bilingual Teachers' Attitudes Toward Mexican American Pupils." S. Diaz, L. C. Moll, and H. Mehan, "Sociocultural Resources in Instruction: A Context-Specific Approach," in Beyond Language: *Social and Cultural Factors in Schooling Language Minority Students* (Los Angeles: California State University, Evaluation, Dissemination and Assessment Center, 1986), pp. 187-230. J. Oaks, "Tracking, Inequality, and the Rhetoric of School Reform: Why Schools Don't Change," *Journal of Education* 168 (1986), pp. 61-80.

26. G. M. Bloom, "The Effects of Speech Style and Skin Color on Bilingual Teaching Candidates' and Bilingual Teachers' Attitudes Toward Mexican American Pupils."

27. A. Lareau. *Home Advantage: Social Class and Parental Intervention in Elementary Education* (New York: Falmer Press, 1990).

28. J. Anyon, "Social Class and the Hidden Curriculum of Work." S. Diaz, L. C. Moll, and H. Mehan, "Sociocultural Resources in Instruction: A Context-Specific Approach." J. Oaks, "Tracking, Inequality, and the Rhetoric of School Reform: Why Schools Don't Change." U.S. Commission on Civil Rights, *Teachers and students: Report V, Mexican American Study: Differences in Teacher Interaction with Mexican-American and Anglo Students* (Washington, DC: Government Printing Office, 1973).

29. S. Diaz, L. C. Moll, and H. Mehan, "Sociocultural Resources in Instruction: A Context-Specific Approach." B. M. Flores, "Language Interference of Influence: Toward a Theory for Hispanic Bilingualism. "B. Flores, P. T. Cousin, and E. Diaz, "Critiquing and Transforming the Deficit Myths About Learning, Language and Culture." S. Sue and A. Padilla, "Ethnic Minority Issues in the US: Challenges for the Educational System," in *Beyond Language: Social and Cultural Factors in Schooling Language Minority Students*, pp. 35-72. H. Trueba "Sociocultural Integration of Minorities and Minority School Achievement," in *Raising Silent Voices: Educating the Linguistic Minorities for the 21st Century* (New York: Newbury House, 1989), pp. 1-27. C. L. Walker, "Hispanic Achievement: Old Views and New Perspectives," in H. Trueba (ed.), *Success or Failure: Learning and the Language Minority Student* (New York: Newbury House, 1987), pp. 15-32.

30. K. H. Au and J. M. Mason, "Cultural Congruence in Classroom Participation Structures: Achieving a Balance of Rights," *Discourse Processes* 6 (1983), pp. 145-168. B. Heath, *Ways with Words* (New York: Cambridge University Press, 1983). H. Mehan "Understanding Inequality in Schools: The Contribution of Interpretive Studies," *Sociology of Education* 65 no. 1 (1992), pp.1-20. S. U. Philips, "Participation Structures and Communication Competence: Warm Springs Children in Community and Classroom," in C. B. Cazden, V. John and D. Hymes (eds.) *Functions of Language in the Classroom* (New York: Teachers College Press, 1972), pp. 370-394.

31. E. G. Cohen, *Designing Groupwork: Strategies for the Heterogeneous Classroom.* C. Edelsky, B. Altwerger, and B. Flores, *Whole Language: What's the Difference?* (Portsmouth, NH: Heinemann, 1991). A. S. Palinscar and A. L. Brown, "Reciprocal Teaching of Comprehension Fostering and Comprehension-Monitoring Activities," Cognition and Instruction 1 no. 23 (1984), pp. 117-175. B. Pérez and M. E. Torres-Guzmán, *Learning in Two Worlds: An Integrated Spanish/English Biliteracy Approach* (New York: Longman, 1992). Zamel, V. "Writing: The Process of Discovering Meaning," *TESOL Quarterly* 16 (1982), pp. 195-209.

32. L. Delpit, *Other People's Children: Cultural Conflict in the Classroom.*

33. "Cultural capital" refers to Bourdieu's concept that certain forms of cultural knowledge are the equivalent of symbolic wealth in that these forms of "high"

culture are socially designated as worthy of being sought and possessed. These cultural (and linguistic) knowledge bases and skills are socially inherited and are believed to facilitate academic achievement. For a more in-depth discussion regarding the multiple meanings of cultural capital in the literature, see M. Lamont and A. Lareau "Cultural Capital—Allusions, Gaps and Glissandos in Recent Theoretical Developments, *Sociological Theory* 6 (1988), pp. 153-168.

34. J. Anyon, "Social Class and the Hidden Curriculum of Work."

35. S. Diaz, L. C. Moll and H. Mehan, "Sociocultural Resources in Instruction: A Context-Specific Approach. L. Moll, "Some Key Issues in Teaching Latino Students," *Language Arts* 65 (1986), pp. 465-472. J. Oaks, "Tracking, Inequality, and the Rhetoric of School Reform: Why Schools Don't Change."

36. P. Freire, *The Politics of Education: Culture, Power and Liberation*, p. 114 (emphasis added).

37. L. Delpit, Other People's Children: Cultural Conflict in the Classroom. M. Reyes, "Challenging Venerable Assumptions: Literacy Instruction for Linguistically Different Students"; "A Process Approach to Literacy During Dialogue Journals and Literature Logs with Second Language Learners," *Research in the Teaching of English* 25 (1991), pp. 291-313.

38. A. M. Villegas, "School failure and Cultural Mismatch: Another View," *Urban Review*, 20 (1988), pp. 253-265; "Culturally Responsible Pedagogy for the 1990s and Beyond," paper prepared for the Educational Testing Service, Princeton, NJ, 1991.

39. K. H. Au and J. M. Mason, "Cultural Congruence in Classroom Participation Structures: Achieving a Balance of Rights," *Discourse Processes* 6 (1983), pp. 145-168. S. B. Heath, Ways with Words. S. U. Philips, "Participation Structures and Communication Competence: Warm Springs Children in Community and Classroom." K. H. Au, "Participant Structures in a Reading Lesson with Hawaiian Children: Analysis of a Culturally Appropriate Event," *Anthropology & Education Quarterly* 11 (1980), pp. 91-115. C. Cazden, *Classroom Discourse: The Language of Teaching and Learning* (Portsmouth, NH: Heinemann, 1988). F. Erickson and G. Mohatt, "Cultural Organization and Participation Structures in Two Classrooms of Indian Students," in G. Spindler (ed.), *Doing the Ethnography of Schooling: Educational Anthropology in Action* (New York: Holt, Rinehart and Winston, 1982), pp. 133-174.

40. K. H. Au, "Using the Experience Text Relationship Method with Minority Children," *The Reading Teacher* 32 (1979), pp. 677-679; "Participant Structures in a Reading Lesson with Hawaiian Children: Analysis of a Culturally Appropriate Instructional Event."

41. K. H. Au and J. M. Mason, "Cultural Congruence in Classroom Participation Structures: Achieving a Balance of Rights." S. B. Heath, *Ways with Words*. S. U. Philips, "Participation Structures and Communication Competence: Warm Springs Children in Community and Classroom." F. Erickson and G. Mohatt,

"Cultural Organization and Participation Structures in Two Classrooms of Indian Students."

42. A. M. Villegas, "School Failure and Cultural Mismatch: Another View."

43. Ibid., p. 260.

44. K. H. Au and J. M. Mason, "Cultural Congruence in Classroom Participation Structures: Achieving a Balance of Rights."

45. H. Giroux, "Introduction," in P. Freire, *The Politics of Education: Culture, Power and Liberation*, p. xxi (emphasis added).

46. L. A. Vogt, C. Jordan & R. G. Tharp, "Explaining School Failure, Producing School Success: Two Cases."

47. R. P. McDermott, "Social Relations as Contexts for Learning in School," *Harvard Educational Review* 47 (1977), pp. 198-213.48. B. F. Jones, A. S. Palinscar, D. S. Ogle, and E. G. Carr, *Strategic Teaching and Learning: Cognitive Instruction in the Content Areas* (Alexandria, VA: Association for Supervision and Curriculum Development, 1987).

49. Ibid., p. 38.

50. R. Avelar La Salle, "The Effect of Metacognitive Instruction on the Transfer of Expository Comprehension Skills: The Interlingual and Cross-Lingual Cases," unpublished doctoral dissertation, Stanford University, 1991. J. S. Hernandez, "Assisted Performance in Reading Comprehension Strategies with Non-English-Proficient Students," *Journal of Educational Issues of Language Minority Students* 8 (1991), pp. 91-112. A. U. Chamot, "How to Plan to Transfer Curriculum from Bilingual to Mainstream Instruction," *Focus*, 12 (1983) (newsletter available from The George Washington University National Clearinghouse for Bilingual Education, 1118 22nd Street NW, Washington, D.C. 20037). J. O'Malley and A. U. Chamot, *Learning Strategies in Second Language Acquisition* (New York: Cambridge University Press, 1990). M. Reyes, "Comprehension of Content Area Passages: A Study of Spanish/English Readers in the Third and Fourth Grade" in S. R. Goldman and H. T. Trueba (eds.), *Becoming Literate in English as a Second Language* (Norwood, NJ: Ablex 1987), pp. 107-126.

51. J. S. Hernandez, "Assisted Performance in Reading Comprehension Strategies with Non-English-Proficient Students."

52. Ibid., p. 101.

53. R. Avelar La Salle, "The Effect of Metacognitive Instruction on the Transfer of Expository Comprehension Skills: The Interlingual and Cross-Lingual Cases."

54. J. Chall, *Stages of Reading Development* (New York: McGraw-Hill, 1983).

55. J. P. Gee, "Literacy, Discourse, and Linguistics: Introduction," *Journal of Education* 171 (1989), pp. 5-17.

56. Ibid., p. 7.

57. For a more detailed discussion of the concept "political clarity," please see L. I. Bartolomé, "Beyond the Methods Fetish: Toward a Humanizing Pedagogy," *Harvard Educational Review* 64, no. 2, Summer (1994), pp. 173-194.

58. "Mainstream" refers to the US macroculture that has its roots in Western European traditions. More specifically, the major influence on the United States, particularly on its institutions, has been the culture and traditions of white, Anglo-Saxon Protestants (WASPs). Although the mainstream group is no longer composed solely of WASPs, members of the middle class have adopted traditionally WASP bodies of knowledge, language use, values, norms, and beliefs.

59. According to Rosaura Sanchez, over 17 million of people in the United States speak Spanish as a first language. See R. Sanchez, "Mapping the Spanish Language Along a Multiethnic and Multilingual Border," in A. Darder & R.D. Torres (eds.), *The Latino Studies Reader: Culture, Economy, and Society* (Malden, MA: Blackwell Publishers, Inc., 1998). According to Conklin and Lourie, the United States has the sixth-largest Spanish-speaking population in the world. See N. F. Conklin and M. A. Lourie, *A Host of tongues: Language communities in the United States,* (New York: The Free Press, 1983).

60. We place quotation marks around the word "foreign" because many of the languages perceived as "foreign" are actually indigenous to geographic areas now part of the United States (for example, the numerous Native American languages and Spanish in the Southwest).

61. Rosaura Sanchez reports that although Latino children constitute 32 percent of all students in the United States (of which approximately two-thirds are limited English proficient), only 10 percent of teachers are Latino. See R. Sanchez, "Mapping the Spanish Language Along a Multiethnic and Multilingual Border."

62. The term "technical" refers to the positivist tradition in education that presents teaching as a precise and scientific undertaking and teachers as technicians responsible for carrying out (preselected) instructional programs and strategies.

63. H. Giroux and P. McLaren, "Politics of Teacher Education," *Harvard Educational Review,* 56, no. 3 (August 1986), pp. 213-238.

64. Giroux and McLaren's definition of transformative intellectual: one who exercises forms of intellectual and pedagogical proactive that attempt to insert teaching and learning directly into the political sphere by arguing that schooling represents both a struggle for meaning and a struggle over power relations. We are also referring to one whose intellectual practices are necessarily grounded in forms of moral and ethical discourse exhibiting a preferential concern for the suffering and struggles of the disadvantaged and oppressed.

65. Taken from the Annual American Educational Research Association Meeting Program, San Diego, California, March, 1998.

66. E. Howard, "Teachers' Beliefs about Effective Educational Practices for Language-Minority Students: A Case Study, qualifying paper, Harvard Graduate School of Education, 1997.

67. R. Gonzalvez, "Resistance in the Multicultural Education Classroom," unpublished manuscript, Harvard Graduate School of Education, 1996, p. 4.

68. Ibid.
69. M. L. Gomez, "Teacher Education Reform and Prospective Teachers' Perspectives on Teaching "Other People's" Children. *Teaching and Teacher Education*, 10, no. 3 (1994), pp. 319-334.
70. National Center for Education Statistics, *American Education at a Glance* (Washington, D.C.: Office of Education Research and Improvement, 1992).
71. N. Zimpher, "The RATE Project: A Profile of Teacher Education Students," *Journal of Teacher Education*, 40, no. 6 (1989), pp. 37-50.
72. B. McLeod, "Introduction," in *Language and Learning: Educating Linguistically Diverse Students* (Albany, NY: SUNY, 1994), p. xiv.
73. See R. Sanchez, "Mapping the Spanish Language Along a Multiethnic and Multilingual Border."
74. S. Nieto, *Affirming Diversity: The Sociopolitical Context of Multicultural Education* (New York: Longman, 1992).
75. P. Bourdieu, "The school as a Conservative Force: Schools and Cultural Inequities," in E. Bredo and W. Fernberg (eds.), *Knowledge and Values in Social and Educational Research* (Philadelphia: Temple University Press, 1982), p. 399.
76. American Association of Colleges for Teacher Education, A*ACTE/Metropolitan Life Survey on Teacher Education Students* (Washington, D.C.: Author, 1990). M. L. Gomez, "Teacher Education Reform and Prospective Teachers' Perspectives on Teaching "Other People's" Children." K. Zeichner and K. Hoeft, "Teacher Socialization for Cultural Diversity," in J. T. Sikula, J. Buttery, and E. Guyton (eds.), *Handbook of Research in Teacher Education*. (New York: MacMillan Library Reference USA, 1986) pp. 525-547.
77. K. A. Davis, "Multicultural Classrooms and Cultural Communities of Teachers," *Teaching and Teacher Education* 11, no. 6 (1995) pp. 553-563.
78. C. E. Sleeter and C. A. Grant, "An Analysis of Multicultural Education in the United States," *Harvard Educational Review* 57 (1987), pp. 421-444. K. Zeichner and K. Hoeft,, "Teacher Socialization for Cultural Diversity."
79. E. E. Sleeter, "Restructuring schools for multicultural education," *Journal of Teacher Education* 43, no. 2 (March-April 1992), pp. 141-148. K. Zeichner and K. Hoeft, "Teacher Socialization for Cultural Diversity."
80. G. Ladson-Billings, "Beyond Multicultural Illiteracy," *Journal of Negro Education* 60, no. 2 (1991), pp. 147-157. R. Alquist, "Position and Imposition: Power Relations in a Multicultural Foundations Class," *Journal of Negro Education* vol. 60, no. 2 (1991), pp. 158-169.
81. Ibid.
82. M. Haberman, "Can Culture Awareness Be Taught in Teacher Education Programs?" *Teacher Education* 4, no. 1 (1991), pp. 25-31.
83. K. Zeichner and K. Hoeft, "Teacher Socialization for Cultural Diversity." M. Haberman, "Can Culture Awareness Be Taught in Teacher Education Programs?"
84. M. Haberman, "Can Culture Awareness Be Taught in Teacher Education Pro-

grams?"; "The Rationale for Training Adults as Teachers," in C. Sleeter (ed.), *Empowerment Through Multicultural Education* (Albany: SUNY Press, 1991), pp. 275-286; *Recruiting and Selecting Teachers for Urban Schools*, (New York: ERIC Clearinghouse for Urban Education, Institute for Urban and Minority Education, 1987).

85. E. Garcia, "Effective Instruction for Language Minority Students: The Teacher," *Boston University Journal of Education* 173, no. 2 (1991); R. T. Jimenez, R. Gersten, and A. Rivera, "Conversations with a Chicana Teacher: Supporting Students' Transition from Native to English Language Instruction," *The Elementary School Journal* 96, no. 3 (1996), pp. 333-341; R. Rueda and H. Garcia "Teachers' Perspectives on Literacy, Assessment and Instruction with Language-Minority Students: A Comparative Study," *The Elementary School Journal* 96, no. 3 (1996), pp. 311-332.

86. P. Freire, Paulo, *Pedagogy of Freedom: Ethics, Democracy, and Civic Courage* (Rowman & Littlefield Publishers, Inc., 1998).

87. Ibid., p. 90.

88. P. Leistyna, *Presence of Mind: Education and the Politics of Deception* (Boulder, CO: Westview Press, 1999).

89. B. Bigelow, "The Human Lives Behind the Labels: The Global Sweatshop, Nike, and the Race to the Bottom," *Rethinking Schools* 11, no. 4 (summer 1997) p. 1.

90. Ibid.

91. Ibid.

92. Ibid., p.12.

93. Ibid.

94. Ibid.

95. P. Freire and D. Macedo, *Literacy: Reading the Word and the World* (South Hadley, MA: Bergin & Garvey Publishers, 1987), p. 132.

96. Refers to informal assessment procedure where readers verbalize all their thought during reading and writing tasks. *See* J. A. Langer, *Children Reading and Writing: Structures and Strategies* (Norwood, NJ: Ablex, 1986), for more in-depth discussion of think-aloud procedures.

97. P. Freire, *A Pedagogy of the City* (New York: Continuum Press, 1993), p. 17.

98. P. Freire, *Pedagogy of Freedom: Ethics, Democracy, and Civic Courage* (Boulder, CO: Rowman & Littlefield Publishers, 1998), p. xx.

INDEX